Tim Boxer's

JEWISH CELEBRITY
Anecdotes

Tim Boxer's
JEWISH CELEBRITY
Anecdotes

JD | JONATHAN DAVID PUBLISHERS, INC.
Middle Village, New York 11379

TIM BOXER'S JEWISH CELEBRITY ANECDOTES

Jonathan David Publishers, Inc.
68-22 Eliot Avenue
Middle Village, New York 11379

2   4   6   7   5   3   1

Library of Congress Cataloging-in-Publication Data

Boxer, Tim
[Jewish celebrity anecdotes]
Tim Boxer's Jewish celebrity anecdotes / by Tim Boxer.
p.cm.
Includes index.
ISBN 0-8246-0391-5
1. Jews—United States—Anecdotes. 2. Celebrities—United States—Anecdotes. I. Title.
E184.J5B7241996
973'.04924—dc2096-17366
CIP

Text design and composition by John Reinhardt Book Design

Printed in the United States of America

In memory of my Uncle Jack Boxer
and in honor of my Aunt Jennie
for their decent and honorable life
that set a model I strive to emulate.

Introduction

I love speeches. Does that seem strange?

I go to dinners and banquets. You know, the kind where they hand out identical plaques for similar service to one cause or another, and then make interminable speeches that have all the black-tie guests squirming in their expensive seats.

Except me. The more they drone on, the more I like it. I sit patiently, listen attentively, make notes cheerfully, and monitor the tape recorder carefully.

You may think this is odd.

You may be right.

Everyone I know goes to these social functions motivated by social and status concerns. They attend because their boss is on the dais or their company bought a table and seats have to be filled. Many go simply to support a worthy charity.

But who goes for the speeches?

I do. And that is the basis of this book. I willingly suffer through endless verbiage in order to winnow out the rare gems and witty thoughts embedded in otherwise boring remarks.

As a columnist for the New York *Jewish Week* and other publications, I cover dinners for worthy causes, benefits for the disease of the week, fund-raising affairs, political functions, and all manner of special events where the main ingredient I seek is not the ubiquitous roast chicken but, believe it or not, the speech.

Really, the after-dinner speech is my stock-in-trade.

I admit I run the risk of terminal boredom. But if I persist I am usually rewarded with a delicious bon mot, a delectable piece of wit and wisdom, an enthralling anecdote, a lovely little story, an amusing tale, a funny one-liner. Over two decades of covering speakers of all stripes and hues for my weekly column, I gleaned a book of stories worth repeating.

Milton Berle forged a career out of stories and gags borrowed from here and there. And you can borrow, too, right from here. (Of course, Uncle Miltie denies he steals jokes. "Occasionally," he says, "I find one that's been lost.")

This book is concise and every story is brief and to the point. That is due to what my wife said. Actually, she says it every night: "Take out the garbage."

From left to right, Gabriel, David, and Nina Boxer.

Before I begin to pass along the wit and wisdom of twenty years on the kosher dinner circuit, I must take a moment to credit Nina Gail, my wife of two decades, who suffered patiently and stoically through innumerable speeches at otherwise entertaining social affairs so that I might achieve my journalistic ends. I am also grateful to my two sons, Gabriel and David, for staying home alone, without complaint, presumably doing their homework, on those many evenings when their parents were out on the town.

Going Public on Chanukah

Shari Lewis knows it is customary to place the *chanukiah** in the window to proclaim the miracle of the season to the world. "I have always been a very public Jew," she says, "but I've never celebrated my heritage so publicly."

That changed dramatically when PBS aired her 1995 television special, *Lamb Chop's Special Chanukah.* "With this show, I am very much putting my menorah in the window."

Shari Lewis and Lamb Chop

When PBS executives came to her with the idea for a prime-time special "to enrich the lives of non-Jewish viewers," the first thing Shari did was call Pat Morita, the Japanese actor and martial arts expert and a close friend, to invite his participation.

"Why not?" Pat said. "After all, I'm half ju and half jitsu."

Then she called another friend, Alan Thicke, star of NBC's *Hope and Gloria*, who said, "How can I do a Chanukah show? I'm not even Jewish!"

"You go to birthday parties and it's not your birthday, right?"

The third guest on the show was Lloyd Bochner, who was raised Orthodox in Toronto. "He helped Pat and Alan understand what's going on," Shari said.

* A nine-candle menorah used specially on Chanukah.

Taking Care of Business

Steve Harris (right) with his wife, Nicole, and the Beatles.

Believe it or not, there was a time when working for the Beatles was a precarious job. There was a chance you might not get paid.

Steve Harris did the marketing and promotion for the moptop quartet before they hit America from the mother country.

"I can't afford you," said manager Brian Epstein.

"Don't worry," Harris said. "I'll send you a bill each week. When you become big in the United States, take care of the bills then."

He did.

First Things First

At the annual dinner of Yeshiva Dov Revel of Forest Hills, New York, Rabbi Nochum Kaplan, the dean, decided to call up Isidore Schindelheim, a longtime supporter, to accept an honor.

The gentleman stepped up and said, "I told them if they spring this on me, I'll walk out—but first I'll eat."

Hot Words Trigger Alarm

"We must end the madness!" declared Israeli Consul General Colette Avital at Israel Bonds' Eleventh Annual Elie Wiesel Holocaust Remembrance Award Dinner, in a moving tribute to Yitzhak Rabin.

Suddenly the fire alarm sounded and tiny strobe lights sparkled in the New York Hilton grand ballroom. The shrieking alarm reminded the audience of Holocaust survivors of those deadly days in concentration camps or the more recent Scud missile attacks on Tel Aviv.

They heard the sirens of the fire trucks. Fear gripped the five hundred dinner guests.

Elie Wiesel

Elie Wiesel, the conscience of the Holocaust, knew exactly what to do. He started to sing "Eliyahu Hanavi," which was quite appropriate, as it was Saturday night, when this hymn in expectation of *moshiach** is traditionally chanted.

Raising his hands like Leonard Bernstein, Wiesel conducted everyone in singing this soothing song of solace. His voice was smooth as velvet.

By the time the singing ended, the false alarm stopped.

* Messiah.

David Ben-Gurion

Can't Satisfy Him

Shimon Peres once characterized David Ben-Gurion as a person who could never be satisfied. "He passed away a dissatisfied person."

He told about the time the old man visited a school in Dimona, where a student asked what was his most satisfied day.

"I never had a satisfied day in my life," the prime minister replied. "A satisfied person is a happy person, and stops dreaming and creating. If you want to remain creative, never be satisfied."

It's All an Act—Or Is It?

Don Wilson, who was Jack Benny's announcer for thirty-five years on radio and television, said Jack wasn't really that stingy. Acting miserly was part of his image.

When Jack played with the Los Angeles Philharmonic, two strings on his fiddle broke. He took them off, carefully rolled them in a neat little ball, and put it in his pocket.

Talk about cheap!

Painting with Words

Larry Miller's standup act contains no one-liners.

"I paint pictures with words," he says. "I am the comic as essayist. It's a way of looking at the world. It's so much in the Jewish tradition. Israel means *God-wrestling*. Jews are unsurpassed for wrestling with the issues."

He illustrates by showing how a Christian and a Jew react when they hear a truth. The Christian crosses his heart. The Jew shrugs his shoulders.

Larry Miller

Everybody's a Doctor

Growing up in the South Bronx, Seymour Kleinman, a corporate lawyer and professional raconteur, wanted to be a doctor. Jews revered doctors, but did not necessarily patronize them. Mama Kleinman would say, "The children were so sick last night I almost called the doctor."

When Sy got sick, Mama would say, "Pull your eyelids three times and spit." That was standard procedure. If that did not work, out came the mustard plasters.

If the ailment persisted, Sy would be sent to Mrs. Moskowitz on the first floor. Never mind that she lacked medical training; her husband was a window washer at Mount Sinai Hospital.

Once Sy's brother Ira swallowed a bunch of aspirin. Mrs. Moskowitz told Sy, "Go upstairs and tell your mother to give Ira a headache."

Painting a New Life in America

Alan King

Alan King's grandfather was Rabbi Harry Solomon. His real name was Dworetsky. When he came to the United States from Poland, he could not get a synagogue position. So he bought a paint store. The name on the store was Solomon. He asked how much it would cost to change the sign. They said fifteen dollars. He said, "Never mind. My name is now Solomon."

You Don't Have to Be Funny

Frank Mancuso, president of Paramount Pictures, was given a formidable assignment by UJA-Federation of New York: say something funny about its guest of honor, Sumner Redstone, chairman of Viacom.

Mancuso was stumped. What was funny about Redstone, a major powerhouse in the entertainment industry?

He did what any shrewd Hollywood executive does when faced with a tough problem. He called a meeting. A roomful of wise men and women sat and thought. They sat and thought for an hour. Then they broke for lunch.

Frustrated, Mancuso decided to seek professional help. He went to see Eddie Murphy.

"You have to say something funny about Sumner Redstone?" an incredulous Eddie exclaimed. "Jason from *Friday the 13th* is funnier than Sumner Redstone!"

Undaunted, Mancuso joined colleagues of different creeds in tribute to the Jewish guest of honor at the dinner. Redstone proved you do not have to be funny to be serious about helping those in need.

Giving Credit Where Due

Ann Miller attributes her initial success in show business to the Jewish people.

This child of Hollywood, as she calls herself, came there at age twelve when her parents divorced. She lied about her age and stayed eighteen for five years.

The first benefit she did was for B'nai B'rith at the Pantages Theater. An agent discovered her there and that night she signed for *New Faces of 1937*, starring Milton Berle.

"I was discovered through B'nai B'rith," she acknowledges. "I got my first contract through them, and whatever I achieved came from the Jewish people."

Ann Miller (center) with Carroll Baker (left) and Blanche Baker.

When You Gotta Go

Richard Boone went to Israel around 1975 to film a western with Jack Palance and Lee Van Cleef. Palance and Cleef were given trailers with bathrooms. Boone got a trailer without a bathroom. So he had a driver take him to Tel Aviv to go to the bathroom. It took four hours. You can bet he got a trailer with a bathroom that day. It was even bigger than the others.

It's a Puzzlement

Ronald Lauder

It is March 1986. Two men, on different continents, are about to set sail on a course in life that will send shock waves around the world.

In the United States, Ronald Lauder, scion of a major cosmetics company, is preparing to go to Vienna as the new ambassador.

In Austria, Kurt Waldheim is gearing up for the presidential elections.

Lauder's telephone rings. It is Waldheim. He is coming to New York. Since he has known the Lauder family for many years and knows that Ronald is going to be the new ambassador, he wants to meet and present him with his new book, *Eye of the Storm*.

The two gentleman have an interesting dinner. Next day, Lauder reads the book. But something puzzles him.

"It's a wonderful book," Lauder tells his Austrian friend. "It starts from 1945. What did you do in the five years before that?"

Waldheim shrugs his shoulders and smiles. "I was on the Russian front. I was wounded in the ankle and spent 1942–1945 in Vienna, studying law."

"How lucky can you be?" Lauder mutters under his breath.

Three days later, Lauder is surprised by a photo of his friend in *The New York Times*. The Austrian is standing tall, resplendent in Nazi uniform. He is identified as a lieutenant in German intelligence in occupied Greece and Yugoslavia. It is 1943.

"This does not look like Vienna," Lauder says to himself.

In this atmosphere of friendly deception, Lauder began his mission as the United States envoy in Vienna, and Waldheim began serving as president of Austria.

On His Best Behavior

Arnold Forster, the longtime counsel to the Anti-Defamation League, was doing radio shows in the 1970s. After taping an interview with Rabbi Shlomo Goren, the chief chaplain of the Israeli army, he asked him to autograph a copy of the army Bible.

"What would a non-Jew want with it?" the rabbi asked.

"But, Rabbi, I am a Jew!"

"Then why have I been polite with you?"

Arnold Forster

Mama Loshen* Sounds Familiar

Ellen Shulman Baker is America's second Jewish astronaut (after the Challenger's Judith Resnick).

As a youngster she went to Bayside High School in Queens. She also went to Talmud Torah, a Hebrew school that she attended in the evening after public school.

One day she told her mother (now Queens Borough President Claire Shulman) that she was studying Yiddish. "I learned *epple*," she said.

"What's that in English?" her mother asked.

"Apple," the kid said.

* "Mother tongue."

How to Make Friends

Marc Weiner and Boney.

Puppeteer Marc Weiner, an observant Jew, once taped an appearance on *The Jim Henson Hour*. He was pleasantly surprised to find kosher food on the lunch break.

"Backstage," Marc says, "I introduced my puppet Rocko to Henson's Muppets. When Rocko told Miss Piggy that he doesn't eat pork, they became instant friends."

Little White Lie

Television producer Norman Lear, who created the megahit *All in the Family*, as well as other extremely popular shows, invited his mother in Bridgeport, Connecticut, to come to the West Coast to celebrate her eighty-fifth birthday. After the visit, as her son the Hollywood mogul was driving her back to the airport, she said, "Norman, if you hear a little white lie from our sisters and relatives, don't worry."

Norman was startled. "What little white lie?"

"It doesn't matter," his mom said. "Why should they know I didn't go to Las Vegas?"

Watch Your Answer

Three days after their honeymoon, Buddy Hackett gets up, and his bride, Sherry, asks, "Should I make breakfast, dear?"

"Don't bother, honeybuns," Buddy says sweetly.

She never asked again.

Buddy Hackett

Fighting Bigotry on Two Fronts

Eli Wallach saw justice visited on prejudice when he was a United States Army medic in Algeria during the Second World War.

German planes would take off from Spain and attack British convoys in the Mediterranean. After each attack the injured English sailors were brought to Eli's base. The commanding officer was a colonel whose hearing was failing. He was a bigot who used to greet Eli every day, "How's President Rosenfelt this morning?"

One day, a British general came to inspect the medical facilities at the base. The general asked, "How often do you change the sheets?" and the colonel answered, "Oh yes, sir, they get three meals a day."

Eli smiled. The colonel's hearing was gone. In a few days the colonel himself, Eli's tormentor, was gone, too.

Invitation to a Banquet

Jan Peerce and his wife, Alice.

Jan Peerce, one of the world's great tenors and favorite opera star, was an observant Jew who kept kosher wherever he traveled. He recalled with a smile the time Joey and Cindy Adams, both converts to Christian Science, hosted a dinner for a mutual friend, Harry Odell. He was a Hong Kong movie tycoon. Chinese artist Dong Kingman was the only non-Jew at the dinner.

"They bring out the first course, a magnificent shrimp," Jan related. "I looked at Cindy and said I can't eat that, I'm kosher. Kingman said he's vegetarian. Odell said he has diabetes. Joey said he has an ulcer. Only Cindy ate the shrimp. The rest of us ended up with a little tuna, an egg, a glass of milk."

What a Garden

Chaim Weizmann was showing a British cabinet member around the Weizmann Institute of Science. They were walking around the campus when the English gentleman remarked, "What a beautiful garden man and the Almighty created."

"You should have seen the place," Weizmann said, "when only the Almighty was the gardener."

Teacher Substitutes to Stardom

Sam Levenson got his start on stage by being at the right place at the right time.

Several school teachers had formed a jazz band to play one summer at Arrowhead Lodge in the Catskills. They promised to bring along a top comedian for the season-ending Labor Day show. But the comic backed out.

Sam and his wife, Esther, were staying at a nearby bungalow. The teachers recalled how he used to regale them with his funny stories at lunchtime at Samuel Tilden High School in Brooklyn where he taught Spanish. So they begged him to substitute for the big name who was a no-show. Sam, who had never been on stage before, wondered if he could do it. They assured him he would be great. Sam went on and brought the house down. The owner booked him for next summer, and Levenson was on his way.

Sam Levenson

Kenst Nit Reddn English?

Screenwriter David Zelig Goodman was walking with his father on Collins Avenue in Miami. His father was talking in Yiddish. Pointing to all the Spanish-speaking immigrants, his father said, "Look at them, speaking Spanish. What's the matter with them? Can't they speak English?" And he was saying that in Yiddish!

Singles Theme Song

Bernie Wayne, composer of *Blue Velvet* and *There She Is, Miss America*, wrote a new theme for singles weekends in the Catskills. He called it *I Came, I Saw, I Concord*.

He also wrote *Laughing on the Outside, Crying on the Inside*. Earl Wilson commented, "A fellow could drown that way."

The Jewish Roots of River Phoenix

Steve North

The tragic death of River Phoenix reminds Steve North of the time in 1988 when he discovered the actor's Jewish roots. Steve, a reporter and producer for Geraldo Rivera, was at that time hosting a radio talk show. He interviewed the promising actor on his eighteenth birthday when he was starring in the Oscar-nominated *Running on Empty*.

"River was an articulate and sensitive person," recalls Steve, who managed to reveal a Jewish angle in most of his guests. "He was totally unaffected by his screen success."

After the program, River and his mother, Arlyn, asked about a vegetarian restaurant. Steve, who belongs to the Reconstructionist Synagogue of the North Shore, on Long Island, recommended the kosher Greener Pastures on the East Side.

"What is kosher?" River asked.

His mother explained what kosher means, which surprised Steve.

"That's when I found out that she's a Jewish woman from the Bronx. River was fascinated with the concept of kosher, and I was fascinated that he was *halachically** a Jew."

---

* In accordance with Jewish law.

Now That's a Friend

Early in his career, Sammy Davis, Jr., owed a debt of gratitude to Milton Berle. When Sammy was appearing with his father and uncle as a singing trio at Ben Maksik's in Brooklyn, he wanted desperately to make the cover of *Our World*, a major black magazine. But he wasn't famous enough.

Davis mentioned this to Berle. The next night Uncle Miltie came and posed with Sammy for a picture. And that's how Sammy got on the cover of the magazine.

Sammy Davis, Jr.

An Unbelievable Scene

Edward R. Murrow came to Kibbutz Sde Boker in the Negev to film a documentary on David Ben-Gurion which aired on CBS in 1956. Israel's first prime minister said, "Too bad you didn't come here three thousand years ago. Moses stood near here and received the Ten Commandments. On television, it would have been for humanity."

After the interview, Murrow was ready to drive off when he realized he had not thanked his host. He stopped the car and went back to the house. He opened the door and saw Ben-Gurion, his back to the door, an apron around his waist, washing the coffee cups.

Murrow's first impulse was to run to the car and get the cameras. Instead he just drove off, realizing that no one would believe they had not set it up.

Kicked into the Butt of Life

Jack Garfein

Jack Garfein, who was artistic director of the Harold Clurman Theater on Forty-second Street and married to Carroll Baker, owes his life to a flick of the wrist from Josef Mengele. Actually it was a swift kick in the butt from a Jewish official at Auschwitz that saved his skin.

When the transport brought thirteen-year-old Jack to the death camp, everyone was divided into two lines. His mother shoved him violently into the line of men. Jack was stunned. He wanted to stay with his mother and sister. He walked up to Mengele.

"How old are you?" Mengele asked.

"I'm sixteen, sir."

A man behind Jack spoke up: "He and I are world famous mosaic artists."

Mengele flicked his wrist, indicating that Jack should go with this man in line. Jack took a step toward the man, then stopped and turned back.

A Jewish kapo could not believe his eyes.

"What are you doing?"

"I want to tell that German officer that I lied," Jack said. "I am not sixteen and I am not a world famous artist."

The kapo struck Jack on the back. He literally kicked the youngster into life. "You stupid Jew!" he shouted as he forced Jack back to the men, who were marched off to slave labor. Jack was the only one of his family to come back alive.

Show Biz Destiny

Bruce Adler was on stage even before he was born. His parents were the Yiddish actors Julius Adler and Henrietta Jacobson. Henrietta was eight months pregnant when she performed in *Who Is Guilty?* in 1945 at the Hopkinson Theater in Brooklyn. She played a grandmother. In a Sabbath scene she sat tight against the table. Suddenly, the table shook, clattering the silverware. The actors were startled, but Henrietta pointed to her stomach—the baby had given a kick.

"I was destined to be an actor," Bruce says.

Bruce Adler

Separate Seating Washington-Style

Julius Berman says when he was chairman of the Conference of Presidents of Major American Jewish Organizations, he was invited to dinner at the State Department. Secretary George Schultz was hosting Israeli Prime Minister Yitzhak Shamir. Berman came with other Jewish leaders.

"The State Department dinner was *glatt* kosher,"* he says. "They even had separate seating. It was Washington style—you sit with my wife, I sit with your wife."

---

* *Glatt* means smooth, the highest degree of kosher. Refers to an animal that has smooth lungs, no scar tissue.

Ghost Story

Folk singer Oscar Brand was flying to Israel with a group. On board he met an accountant from Philadephia who said he and his wife used to come to all his concerts. Where is his wife? She was in baggage. The man was bringing her body for burial in the Holy Land.

At Ben-Gurion Airport, the man couldn't find his friend who was supposed to meet him. Oscar offered a lift in one of two vans that his party had rented. The man hoisted his steamer trunk on the roof of the van and took off for Jerusalem. Oscar followed a short time later in the second car.

He came upon the man standing on the highway next to his van. The steamer trunk had fallen off the car. Some Arabs tossed it into their car and fled in the opposite direction.

The man never acknowledged the lost trunk. "Apparently he sneaked the body of his wife illegally into the country," Oscar says.

"Somewhere that day, some Arabs eagerly opened their trunk stolen from an American tourist and, instead of finding riches, they came face to face with a corpse."

GEORGE PICKOW

Oscar Brand

Mother's Advice

David Mitchell, addressing the National Political Action Committee at Peter Max's studio near Lincoln Center, came equipped with maternal advice.

His mother told him three things:

Stand tall so you can be seen.
Speak loud so you can be heard.
Step down so you can be appreciated.

Who Made Out Better?

Bender Solomon, a retired judge from Albany, New York, was reminiscing with his wife, Mildred, and friends at the Concord Resort Hotel. Someone mentioned Abbe Lane and Mildred recalled when they were neighbors in the Bronx.

She said Abbe Lane was born Frances Lassman in Brooklyn. Her father was a window trimmer, her mother a milliner. Frances was three years old when the family moved to the Bronx. Frances and Mildred grew up in the same apartment building at 190 West 170th Street.

"Frances was a very smart child," Mildred said. "She wasn't the least shy. She was born with natural talent. She sang and danced. She spent more time in our apartment than in her own.

"My mother told her mother to take her for dance lessons. Frances went to the Jack Blue dance school. He taught Ruby Keeler and Patsy Kelly. He put the six-year-old Frances on the *Horn & Hardart Amateur Hour*."

Mildred ran into Abbe Lane's mother many years later in Miami. Mrs. Lassman told her, "You married a judge–you did better!"

Singing Their Way to Safety

Lillian Lux

Lillian Lux and her late husband, Pesach Burstein, were shining stars of the Yiddish stage in the thirties. In 1939 they played at the prestigious La Scala in Warsaw. It was 1939 and the smell of war was in the air. The American consul was a fan of Pesach. He had seen him perform in Philadelphia where he attended law school. He warned Pesach to return to the United States at once. The only ship leaving for America was sold out. Pesach pleaded with the captain, saying he will give two concerts if he would let them come aboard.

Pesach and Lillian gave a concert on September 1. After the performance, the captain announced that Germany had attacked Poland.

"People cried all the way to New York," Lillian says. "We grieved for those we left behind—Pesach's sister, nieces and nephews."

Tryout in the Temple

Martin Charnin, the lyricist for the Broadway musical *Annie*, tells a story about composer Harold Arlen. Harold's father was a cantor in Buffalo. He would send his father melodies which he was considering making into songs. The father would interpolate these tunes into the Shabbat davening. If the congregation approved, he would tell his son to go ahead and write the song.

Shakespeare in Yiddish

Shakespeare, especially *King Lear*, was a favorite of the Yiddish theater. Once when Walter Matthau was in a taxi in New York, the driver asked in his heavy Yiddish accent, "Aren't you an actor?"

"Yes."

"What are you doing?"

"I'm playing King Lear on Broadway."

"Really? Do you think it would go in English?"

Walter Matthau

Early Sound Effects

Yehuda Efroni recalls the hard times that actors had in Israel's early years. For instance, they had to improvise their own sound effects.

"We had an old retired actor offstage who would bang a broom handle on a chair to simulate the sound of a gunshot. Once I had to commit suicide in a play. I put the gun to my head and pulled the trigger. No sound. The old man had fallen asleep.

"Quickly, I threw the gun away and took a dagger. I aimed for my heart and struck. There was a gunshot sound. The old man had awakened."

The Big Payoff

Ed Koch, New York's former mayor, relates a sardonic incident when he was a Congressman. He was invited by Howard Squadron, then president of the American Jewish Congress, to speak gratis at the Connecticut home of Theodore Bikel.

"I don't like to travel out of New York City—I get the bends. But I gave up a Saturday night to go there. There were forty heavy hitters, big contributors to the organization, and I was the guest attraction.

"They began reading the cards, calling names, and each one responded with $25,000 donations. Suddenly I heard my name: Congressman Koch, what will you be contributing?

"It was embarrassing. Here I was invited to speak. I certainly didn't think they would be calling on me to donate also. So I said, 'I'm contributing my honorarium, which is always $5,000.'"

Ed Koch

Is It the Right Size?

Moshe Dworkin, vice president of Bnai Zion, recalls the time the Soviets replaced Andrei Vishinski with Andrei Gromyko at the United Nations. A press release went out with the head, "Gromyko Steps into Vishinski's Shoes." The Kremlin got upset with the headline, fearing that people in the United States would think Soviet diplomats had only one pair of shoes.

Who's Birthday—Moses?

When their two sons were backpacking with eight other kids in Europe, Saul Turteltaub and his wife flew over to join them in Paris. Saul, a television producer, keeps a kosher home in Los Angeles.

As it was Passover, Saul and his wife brought all the seder ingredients—*charoses,** *maror,*** a hardboiled egg, a shankbone—packed in ice in a thermal bag. Also *yarmulkes* and *haggadas.** They ordered fish and vegetables from room service at the Plaza Athenee.

The waiter arranged the food on the *Seder* table, then walked to the door and said, "Happy Birthday!"

Saul Turteltaub

Now You See What's in a Name

Because he was appearing at Westbury Music Fair, Buddy Hackett had to miss the *brit*** of his first grandchild. The boy was born to his daughter in Denver.

"They named him Joshua Philip Miller," Buddy said. "Philip is my father's name. Joshua must be the name of my son-in-law's father. If he had named my grandson Philip first, I would have given him $25,000. Now I'll just give him a bicycle."

---

*   A paste made from apples, spices, nuts, and wine that is used as part of the *Seder*. It
      represents the mortar used by the Hebrews to make bricks during their slavery in Egypt.
**   Bitter herbs.
*   Literally "narration," the book used at the *Seder* service to recite the story of Exodus.
**   Circumcision ceremony.

Jose Ferrer

Checking It Out

Jose Ferrer was not Jewish but was a great fan of Menashe Skulnick. He used to go down to Second Avenue to see him perform. But he never met the Yiddish actor in person.

When Ferrer was starring in Arthur Miller's *After the Fall*, he got a visitor one day. Skulnick, who was to star in the next show, *The Fifth Season*, came to Ferrer's dressing room.

Skulnick came in, walked here and there, looked around, muttered "Yes, it will do," and walked out.

Chicken Needs a Rabbi, Not a Doctor

Yashar Hirshaut, head of the Israel Cancer Research Fund, is both a doctor and a rabbi. This poses a problem for people who greet him. Do you call him Doctor Hirshaut or Rabbi Hirshaut?

He says this reminds him of the woman in Germany who was not sure if her chicken was kosher. She brought it to her rabbi who, like many clergy, also had a Ph.D.

"Is the rabbi home?" the woman asked.

"The doctor is not home," the wife replied.

"When will the rabbi be home?"

"I'm afraid I cannot say when the doctor will be home."

"May I come in and wait for the rabbi?"

"You may wait for the doctor."

"Listen," the exasperated woman said, "this chicken is already dead. What it needs is a rabbi."

The Lonely Writer

Cynthia Ozick, who has written such books as *The Pagan Rabbi and Other Stories* and *The Cannibal Galaxy*, wondered why she was chosen for "an award for meritorious service to Jewish communal life" by the Writers and Artists for Peace in the Middle East.

"I belong to no communal organizations. I go to no meetings. I sit at a table alone, mostly at night, and press out mostly unsatisfactory words. A Jew is most actively a Jew in a quorum of Jews. One must be a member of a community. How then can a lonely writer deserve a communal award?"

Cynthia Ozick

You Gotta Know Someone

Ellen Radner, a cousin of Gilda Radner, came to Los Angeles as a single woman from Detroit. She taught English as a second language at the University of Southern California. Being single, she wanted to join the show biz *shul*,* Synagogue for Performing Arts, which she heard so much about. They turned her down because membership was restricted to people working in the entertainment industry.

"Three years later I got even with them," she says, "I married David Baron, and he became rabbi of the synagogue."

* Synagogue.

No Time to Waste

Freddie Roman

On his trip to Israel, Freddie Roman had a very enthusiastic guide. He went twenty-two hours straight. Freddie wanted to take a nap, but the guide insisted, "You can't. I have more to show you."

When in Rome

There is a non-Jewish resident at the Jewish Home and Hospital for the Aged in Manhattan who wears a *yarmulke*.

Why?

"I get a better lunch!" he quipped.

Synagogue Seats are Expensive

Monty Hall lovingly recalls his youth in Winnipeg, where his family attended Bais Yaacov Shul. He says six persons occupied three seats on the High Holidays. How was that possible?

"Easy. In the typical Orthodox synagogue in those days, half the men would walk up and down the aisles visiting their neighbors, shmoozing with their associates, with people telling them *sha shtill*.* That explains how six of us occupied three seats. And that's how the term *wandering Jew* began."

* Shh, quiet.

Cleaning Up to Get a Job

At age fifteen, Jamie Masada left his home in Jerusalem to seek his fortune in Hollywood. An agent sent him on an interview for a small part as a porter on the *Colombo* television series. Jamie showed up at the producer's office, said he was the porter and immediately got a job—cleaning the office.

Jamie stayed there cleaning all day, thinking that is what he had to do to get a television role. At the end of the day, after Jamie had cleaned the office several times over, the producer finally realized that his porter was really an actor, and gave him a part in an episode of his TV series.

In due time Jamie opened the Laugh Factory, a popular comedy club which *Fortune* cited as one of the "sophisticated Hollywood warehouses stuffed with celebrities and nonstop comedy."

Jamie Masada

He Can Believe It

Menachem Begin's right-hand man, Yechiel Kadishai, was guest of honor at a party of American Friends of Assaf Harofeh Medical Center. The praise was gushing from speaker after speaker.

"The difference between this kind of tribute and a eulogy at a funeral," Kadishai observed, "is that in this room there is at least one person who believes what is said."

Watch What You Say to Kids

Abe Vigoda

"I always suggest to parents to be careful what they say to children," says Abe Vigoda, who portrayed Sal Tessio in *The Godfather*. "They do understand and they do remember."

Abe remembers vividly when he was six years old and the teacher was forming a drama class. The teacher needed someone to play Baron von Richenhoffen, a fifty-year-old man who finds his wife in the closet with a strange man. She looked around the room and stopped at little Abe.

"You look old," the teacher said. "You'll do for the part."

"At six she said I looked old," Abe says. "I've been playing old ever since."

Speaking without End

Rabbi Stephen Wise, founder of the American Jewish Congress, was one of the great orators of his time. A young rabbi, who saw Wise in the audience, wanted to impress him. So he spoke eloquently but endlessly.

After his speech, the young man was eager to get Wise's opinion of his oratory.

"Young man," Wise said, "there is one thing you must learn. A sermon need not be eternal to be immortal."

Setting Sights on Broadway

When George S. Irving was still in high school in Springfield, Massachusetts, he would hitchhike to New York. He would stay with relatives in Williamsburg and go to Manhattan to look at the Broadway theaters. He could not afford to go in—he would just look.

"My father always told me to eat in a dairy restaurant," he says. "Anywhere else you'll get poisoned. Meat can spoil. Who can spoil a bowl of borscht?"

Soon after he moved to New York, George became a bass soloist with the Samuel Sterner Symphonic Choir, appearing at the Mount Eden Synagogue in the Bronx and Grossinger's during the holidays.

George shudders as he recalls the stern hand of Sterner. He would yell, "Sing on pitch, Goldberg! You're tearing my heart out!"

George S. Irving

Poor Goldberg was only nine years old.

"It was good discipline," George says. "The music I learned then has stayed with me to this day and helped me in my musical theater career."

Born with Street Smarts

Comedian Martin Rudow came to New York from Milwaukee and got an apartment in a tough neighborhood. To secure his apartment, he put six locks on the door. But he would lock only three of them.

"I figured if a burglar picks the locks, he'll open three and lock three."

Is that a *Yiddishe kohp** or what?

---

* Jewish smarts. Literally, "Jewish head."

Mark of a Star

A highlight of the Barry Sisters' career came when they appeared with Mickey Katz on Broadway. Al Hirschfeld made a caricature of the girls for *The New York Times*. Claire was so excited she called her father with the great news.

There was a long silence.

"Are you there, daddy?"

"Yes, I'm here. Listen, if you tell me your picture is in *The Forward*, that tells me something. That means you are a star. But what do I know from *The New York Times*?"

SIDNEY GLUCK

Al Hirschfeld

Check His Passport

As John Zuccotti, president of the Olympia & York realty empire, accepted the Irvin Feld Humanitarian Award from the National Conference of Christians and Jews, he was reminded of a Martin Buber story.

Buber said that Christians believe the Messiah walked on the earth and they await his second coming. Jews believe he has not come yet, and await his first arrival.

So Buber advised that we all just wait until the Messiah comes. Then ask him, "Have you ever been here before?"

Zuccotti, however, cautioned that the Messiah should answer tactfully, "I can't remember."

The Measure of Fame

Eddie Fishbaum found out what fame really is.

When his friend David Mizrahi was leaving on a trip to Israel, Eddie gave him a special type of microphone to bring to singer Avi Toledano in Tel Aviv.

At Kennedy Airport, Mizrahi opened his bags for inspection. Then he said he had another bag.

"What's in it?" the inspector asked.

"A microphone. I'm delivering it for a friend."

"Who gave it to you?"

"Eddie Fishbaum."

"Eddie Fishbaum? The owner of Broadway's Jerusalem II Pizza?"

"Yes."

"Go ahead, you don't have to open it."

Eddie Fishbaum

Thank You, but No

Abba Eban recalls the early days of statehood, when Israel was barely producing enough food for its people.

Burma, among the very first to recognize the fledgling state, wanted to send President Chaim Weizmann a gift of a ten-ton elephant. You can imagine how much food that beast would have diverted from the hard-pressed populace.

The president asked his aide, Eban, to compose a note of refusal.

"In our small Russian town of Motol," Weizmann explained, "the custom was never to accept a gift that eats."

Dancing Her Way Up

Jackie Angelescu came from Romania and, at age twelve, is already making her mark in show business. She's a dancer in the Rodgers and Hammerstein musical *State Fair* on Broadway. Jackie says she has encountered no anti-Semitism. But when her mother, Sarina, worked as an accountant, she heard an occasional barb.

Someone remarked. "The whole economy is wrong. It's all the fault of the Jews."

"The Jews and the bicycle people," Sarina said.

"Why the bicycle people?" the person asked.

"Why the Jews?" Sarina asked.

Dinner—Whether You Like It or Not

Alan King says his mother and father hated each other. They would never talk to each other. His mother would always talk about his father, and his father would always talk about his mother–even if they were in the same room.

Alan remembers his mother saying, "Tell your father dinner is ready."

"Ma," Alan said, "he's sitting right there. Why don't you tell him?"

"I wouldn't give him the satisfaction."

Alan turned to his father. "Ma says dinner is ready."

"Tell her I don't eat that junk!"

Alan said, "Ma . . ."

"I heard him!" she snapped.

Going in Opposite Directions

Robert Merrill and Frank Sinatra are longtime buddies. Francis marvels at Bob's voice. "I'm jealous," he said. "Bob sings better and louder than I do."

To which Bob's wife Marion responded, "Don't worry. He still can't be a saloon singer."

They became friends when both won the Major Bowes Amateur Hour contest on radio. Ol' Blue Eyes became a bobbysox idol and performed at the Paramount. Bob appeared five blocks away at the Metropolitan Opera House.

"To do operas," Bob said, "I had to learn Italian, French, German. What did my friend learn? Doo be doo be doo!"

Robert Merrill (right) with his wife, Marion, and Frank Sinatra.

Getting His Priorities Straight

Mario Cuomo was governor of New York when he appointed a retired rabbi, Israel Mowshowitz, as assistant for community affairs. The governor introduced him in Albany.

"This is my rabbi," Cuomo said to Bishop Hubbard.

"The governor calls me his rabbi," Mowshowitz said, "but he pays his dues to you."

Leon Charney's Strategy
with Frank Sinatra

Frank Sinatra once sued Earl Wilson—and Hebrew University came out the winner.

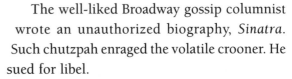

Leon Charney

The well-liked Broadway gossip columnist wrote an unauthorized biography, *Sinatra*. Such chutzpah enraged the volatile crooner. He sued for libel.

Wilson ran scared. "I need a lawyer," he told me, his assistant. "Get Leon Charney," I said.

Charney formed a strategy whereby he had the right to take Sinatra's deposition.

"My feeling," Charney says, "was that Sinatra would not make himself available for a deposition because, in a sense, we could ask the same questions he was suing Wilson on. He was saying that Wilson made statements that were not true. I would ask him what is the truth. I would ask whether he was in love with Ava Gardner or not, plus questions concerning his relationship with Juliet Prowse and Mia Farrow. I had my doubts that he would sit for such an interview. His answers would cause a media sensation."

A date was set for the deposition. Charney flew out to Los Angeles to meet the singer's lawyer, the invincible and fearsome Mickey Rudin. They rode in Rudin's Rolls Royce to Sinatra's home in Palm Springs to take the deposition.

Charney kept wondering if his strategy was going to work. "Rudin sounded like a teamster from Hoboken," Charney says. "He kept a cigar in his mouth. I told him I hate cigar smoke and could he please put it out. He glared at me. It's his car and who am I to tell him what to do. But then he put down the cigar."

At that moment Charney knew he had won the case. "Because," he says, "if Rudin did not really want to accommodate me, he would have dropped me in the middle of the desert and tell me to take a cab."

Sinatra settled. "The settlement is secret," Charney says, "so I can't talk. But Sinatra and Wilson agreed that the beneficiary would be Hebrew University."

It Was a Tight Squeeze

Jazz songstress Sylvia Syms wanted to take her mother, Pauline Blagman, out for her ninety-second birthday.

"Mama's home was always *glatt* kosher," Sylvia said. "She lived in her own apartment. She's a *balabusteh*."*

Sylvia called a kosher Chinese restaurant in Brooklyn, Shang Chai. "Can you hold a table for three?" she asked.

"I'll squeeze you in," the hostess said.

"We came and the place was empty," Sylvia said with a hearty laugh.

Sylvia Syms

TIM BOXER

* Yiddish version of the Hebrew *baal habayis*, "head of the household."

Sammy Davis, Jr.

Taking Deadly Aim

After rehearsing at the Concord Resort Hotel, Sammy Davis, Jr., was sitting in his room looking glum. A cap had fallen off a tooth. How could he go on stage?

No problem. With 2,500 people in the world-famous hotel, they easily found a dentist, on the tennis court, who put the cap back in place and saved the show.

While singing *Bojangles*, Sammy started to whistle. The dentist, seated ringside, grew nervous. "I thought he might hit someone on the head with that cap," he said.

Depends Where You Are

Henny Youngman met a friend at a Catskills resort. "What are you doing here?" he asked. "I'm the *shochet*,* " the friend said.

Later in the season, Henny ran into the same man in Miami Beach. "What are you doing in Miami Beach?" The friend said, "Here, I'm the golf pro."

Permanent Position

Yoram Aridor gave up his post as finance minister to represent Israel at the United Nations. He said he liked his new status.

"The title of minister of finance is a temporary title," he said. "But the title of former minister of finance is a permanent title."

* A person certified to slaughter animals in accordance with Jewish law.

It Went Right to His Head

Jack Lemmon always loved Israeli military headgear. When he appeared in *Long Day's Journey into Night* in Tel Aviv, he went out to plant a tree. He admired the young soldiers with their distinctive berets. He asked his friend, attorney Leon Charney, to get him a couple of the berets to take home.

Charney took Lemmon to see his pals at the Ministry of Defense. That night an officer arrived backstage and presented the actor with seven berets, representing the various military corps. The gift went right to Lemmon's head.

In Los Angeles, Lemmon wrote to Charney: "I enjoyed our time together in Tel Aviv immensely and I'm going to eat out for a month on our visit to the Ministry of Defense. Would you believe that terrific young man showed up at the theater that night with a brand new beret for every division of the army that there is, plus a couple of others that I think he made up. Have we got hats!"

Leon Charney (left) and Jack Lemmon.

There's a Line for Everything

Attorney Louis Nizer said that in the early days of statehood, Israelis had to stand on endless lines for food. One day a man got so fed up he left the line, saying he was going to shoot the prime minister. Half an hour later he came back.

"What happened?" they asked.

"There was a line," the man said.

Louis Nizer

Camp David Odd Couple

New York attorney Leon Charney helped broker the Egyptian-Israeli peace treaty by serving as Jimmy Carter's liaison with Menachem Begin at the Camp David negotiations.

Atlanta attorney Robert Lipshutz, who was White House counsel, explained how he and Leon got the chutzpah to become so involved in affairs of state.

In Robert's case, the impetus came from two sources: "The teachings of our Jewish religion and my appreciation for the United States, where my grandparents came as refugees escaping from czarist Russian oppression a hundred years ago."

The legal team of Lipshutz and Charney served their country well. As Lipshutz puts it: "This courtly Southern gentleman and this brash young man from Bayonne became known at Camp David as the Odd Couple."

What's the Matter with You?

Wayne Rogers, who was Trapper John in *M*A*S*H* on television, once went to the bar mitzvah of a friend's son at a synagogue on Wilshire Boulevard. The non-Jewish actor found the service rather lengthy. He turned to his son and said, "Bill, let's go."

The four-year-old said, "Dad, I don't want to go."

Two men leaned over and admonished Rogers, "What's the matter with you? You taking a kid out of temple?"

Making Out Okay

Agent Kenny Grayson picked up Henny Youngman in his compact car at Grossinger's and drove him to the Raleigh for the late show. Henny was a tall fellow.

"Henny," the agent asked, "are you comfortable?"

"I make a nice living," the comedian replied.

Henny Youngman

Lauren Bacall

Such Close Friends

Kirk Douglas and Lauren Bacall started out as students at the American Academy of Dramatic Arts. Of course, in their early years they were known as Issur Danielovich Demsky and Betty Joan Perske. To make ends meet, Kirk worked as a waiter at Schrafft's on the West Side. Lauren got an overcoat from an uncle and gave it to Kirk, who wore it for two years.

Later Lauren got Kirk his first acting job by recommending him for the film *The Strange Loves of Martha Ivers* in 1946.

"We've had a unique relationship all these years," Lauren said. "I never see him."

You're the Boss

When he came to New York on his semi-annual visit, El Al president Rafi Harlev said his taxi ride from Kennedy Airport was as long as his flight from Tel Aviv.

He praised his flight as quite smooth but admitted that service could use improvement.

"El Al attendants smile when they feel like it. If they hate you, their faces show it. They have their ups and downs. Service runs hot and cold.

"When you board an El Al plane, you feel it belongs to you. You feel like you paid for it. You don't have that feeling with any other airline."

An Overnight Sensation

Jackie Mason had long ago made up his mind that "I will never pass from this life with money in my pocket."

That was not hard to do.

He was kicked off *The Ed Sullivan Show*. He produced his own play that flopped, and a movie that nobody came to see. He borrowed money from his sister and others.

"Then one day I was doing nothing and became a hit," he marveled. He opened *The New York Times* and read a smashing review of his one-man Broadway show and has been enjoying phenomenal success ever since.

Jackie Mason

Kindness of a Stranger

Before Jack Garfein became an artistic director of the Harold Clurman Theater on Forty-second Street and husband of Carroll Baker, he was a survivor of eleven concentration camps. When he was liberated by the British, he was fourteen and weighed forty-eight pounds. (Hebrew Immigrant Aid Society) brought him to America.

He was hungry. He walked the streets of New York looking at the menus in cafeterias trying to see where he could get soup with bread for a nickel. He was looking through the window of a restaurant when a man came out and said, "Get in here. I know a hungry face when I see one."

Jack went in and studied the menu for the cheapest item he could buy. The owner said, "Order anything you want. He left enough to pay for it."

Returns to His Heritage

Werner Klemperer

Werner Klemperer, who played Col. Klink on television's *Hogan's Heros*, was born in Cologne, Germany, to a Jewish father and Lutheran mother. His father, Otto Klemperer, was head of the Cologne Opera House and later music director of the Berlin State Opera. At age twenty Otto converted to Catholicism and that is how he brought up his son.

The Klemperers were staunch Germans, devoted to German civilization. Nevertheless, as the Nazis began marching and the streets turned unsafe for Jews, Otto took his son out of school. The family found refuge in America, where Otto was conductor for many years of the Los Angeles Philharmonic.

At age eighty-two, the world renowned conductor renounced his conversion and returned to his people. Werner isn't quite certain why his father came back to the faith to which he was born.

"My father was always interested in religion," Werner said. "He wanted to return to his heritage."

Maid Learns Torah

Alan King was always disappointed that his son never finished studying for his bar mitzvah. "For three years the tutor taught him the *haftorah.** Every day, all we heard was the *haftorah.* For three years he couldn't learn it, couldn't understand it. Even the maid learned it. But not my kid."

---

* Selection from the Prophets read by the bar mitzvah following the reading of the Torah.

Where Were the People?

Linda Lavin played a heroine of the Holocaust when she starred in the television drama *Lena: My 100 Children.* She portrayed Lena Kuchler-Silberman, a teacher who managed to survive the Nazi scourge in Poland. After the war Lena found a hundred starving children in an abandoned orphanage in Cracow. She nursed them back to health and brought them to a new life in Israel.

"It makes me feel heroic to play such a person," Linda said. But it wasn't until she met one of the survivors that Linda understood how important a role she had played.

"I went through hell," Rose Schimmel of Queens, New York, told Linda.

Linda Lavin

Rose said she was six when war came to her village on the Ukrainian-Polish border. The Ukrainians, supposed friends of the family, chased her uncle into the woods and "shot him like a dog." They also murdered her father and brother. She hid in a trench in the forest with her mother for a week before she realized her mother was dead.

Rose told Linda that she was puzzled. If a disaster happens in the United States, people respond with help from all over.

"How come nobody came to help me? I was left an orphan, a little girl. Where were the people? I mean, nobody heard our cry? Didn't people know what was going on?"

Tell a Woman and You Tell the World

Estée Lauder (right) and her son,
Ambassador Ronald Lauder.

Estée Lauder credits Hadassah for a big boost in her cosmetics business. She explains that many years ago, in response to a friend's request, she donated her best lipstick in gold cases for a Hadassah dinner.

The next morning she got seventy phone calls from women asking for similar donations of merchandise for various other events.

"I found," she says, "that there are three ways to send a message to the world: telephone, telegraph, tell a woman."

Joining the Minyan

Author Sidney Zion was sitting in a restaurant with Frank Sinatra. Sidney mentioned going to the Actors Temple every night to say *Kaddish** for his father, who had died at age eighty.

"Do you have trouble getting a *minyan?*"** the Chairman of the Board asked.

Sidney said sometimes he had to collar people on the street to make up a quorum. Next day a limousine pulled up on West Forty-seventh Street. Out popped Ol' Blue Eyes and his pal, Father Rooney. They donned *yarmulkes* and joined the congregation for *maariv.**

*   The prayer recited by mourners.
** A religious quorum of ten men.
*   "Evening" (Hebrew), the third of three prayer services during the day.

His Most Embarrassing Moment

Red Buttons was so thrilled to sign on for a role in the James Cagney film *13 Rue Madeleine*, he ran to Lindy's to tell the gang. Milton Berle, Jack E. Leonard, Jan Murray, and all the other regulars were happy for him. His mother packed some chicken fat sandwiches for the train ride to Quebec, where filming would take place.

When he stepped off the train, casting director Meyer Mishkin told him to get back on and go home—his scenes had been cut. How could he face the boys at Lindy's? Red pleaded for a small part, anything.

On the set, Cagney, who spoke a pretty good Yiddish, recognized Red from burlesque and called him "Hey, Roite." They conversed in Yiddish, and Cagney asked the director to find Red a part in the picture.

Red Buttons

Watch the scene where Cagney bails out of the airplane in occupied France. That's Red standing by to signal him to jump by saying "Go."

All the comics gave Red a hearty welcome home at Lindy's. The day the movie opened at the Roxy, the whole gang rushed over to meet in the balcony, armed with sandwiches from the Stage Delicatessen. They were impatient to see Red's debut on the big screen.

Red, by now thoroughly embarrassed, sat downstairs, alone.

The big scene came, and from Red's mouth came his only line of dialogue. From the balcony a murmur began.

"Go?" exclaimed Jack E. Leonard.

"Go?" cried Milton Berle.

A whole chorus of "Go?" thundered from the crowd.

As Red sauntered into Lindy's, all his colleagues raised the cry "GO!" Red could never live that down.

Not Fit to Sell

Broadway composer Albert Hague was in Los Angeles acting in the television series *Fame*. One day, while doing a scene downtown, he saw a newsstand stocked with *The New York Times* and *Variety*.

"I was so overjoyed to see a hometown newspaper that I ran over to buy a couple of copies," he said. "They wouldn't sell. Turns out it was a fake newsstand for the scene we were filming."

Albert Hague

A Club that's Restricted

In the 1920s, some forty millionaires in New Jersey started the Aldecress Country Club, one of the finest and toughest golf courses in the country. It was located in the vicinity of Alpine, Demarets and Cresskill (from which the name was derived).

The club was within walking distance from Donald Flamm's house in Closter. Donald was the owner of radio station WMCA in New York. In 1939 he applied for membership. He was turned down—no Jews were welcome.

The club fell on hard times in the '40s and went on the auction block after the war. Donald bought it dirt cheap and developed it into the highly successful Alpine Country Club.

"Newspaper people asked me if I was going to continue the restrictive policy," Donald related. "I said yes—restricted to people of good will."

The club flourished from 1946 to 1960 when Milton Berle was a regular.

He Acts Jewish

Rod Steiger went to Israel for the premiere of *The Pawn-broker*, in which he starred as the Holocaust survivor. His Israeli hosts wanted to honor him with the lighting of a flame in memory of the Holocaust victims.

He balked because he wasn't Jewish and did not wish to desecrate.

A rabbi asked, "You did *The Pawnbroker*?"

"Yes."

"You're Jewish. Light the candle."

Rod Steiger

TIM BOXER

That's Hollywood

Lorne Greene was one of the first in a wave of Canadian actors to invade Los Angeles in the Fifties. At a cocktail party at the time, talk centered on the House Un-American Activities Committee searching for Communists.

"The Russians have nothing on us," Greene said. "What we have to fear is the takeover by Canadians. Half of Hollywood is run by Canadians."

Greene, best known as Ben Cartwright on *Bonanza*, was once married to a woman named Rita. The rabbi who officiated at the wedding was the distinguished Reform leader, Maurice Eisendrath. When they divorced, Rita married the rabbi.

Sammy Cahn

Alive After All

Sammy Cahn, the prolific lyricist, said that whenever Frank Sinatra asked him who wrote a specific song, he'd say Menashe Skulnik.

Ol' Blue Eyes always was convinced it was a made-up name, a sort of in-joke.

One day he was in a limousine on Second Avenue when he shouted, "Stop the car!" He jumped out in front of a theater full of excitement. He looked up at the sign and cried, "There is a Menashe Skulnik!"

Taking the Plunge

It was 1946, at a nightclub where aspiring comedians were trying out for a spot in the limelight, when Broadway columnist Earl Wilson spotted Sam Levenson. Sam was a thirty-four-year-old Brooklyn high school teacher. Earl was impressed that he did not stoop to dirty jokes or dialect, as some of the other fledgling comics did to get cheap laughs.

Sam was hesitant about taking the plunge and becoming a standup comic. But Earl encouraged him: "I'm a Methodist from Ohio, but I see myself and people I grew up with in the stories you tell."

Singing to Get It Right

In his fabulous show at the Concord Resort Hotel, Anthony Newley sang *What Kind of Fool Am I*. It was a song he wrote with composer Leslie Bricusse and which Sammy Davis, Jr., recorded into a monster hit.

"I sing it every night of my life," he said. "I never get tired of it because I never know when I will get it right."

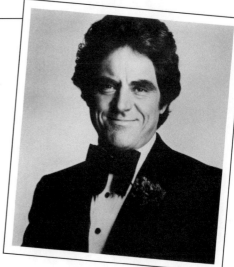

Anthony Newley

Arms to Israel

Meyer Lansky never forgave Israel for refusing to let him settle there. Joel Gross, author of *The King's Daughter*, a novel focusing on how the Mafia helped ship weapons to the newly created State of Israel, said that Lansky felt he helped the emerging state immensely by arranging for New York longshoremen to ship the arms.

"Those crates of weapons," Gross said, "were destined for Egypt. Lansky got the dockworkers to stamp the crates 'Industrial Equipment' and redirect the shipment to Haifa.

"The Jews couldn't acquire arms because of the British blockade. The Arab countries obtained all the weapons they wanted. The British themselves sent arms to Jordan. Seven Arab countries were getting arms, but not the Jews.

"The longshoremen, mostly Irish, were happy to go along with Lansky because they would do anything against the British."

Joey Bishop

Just One Picture

Joey Bishop says he was walking on the Boardwalk in Atlantic City when a fan ran over with his wife and three children.

"Joey Bishop!" he cried. "Please, just one picture."

"My pleasure," Joey said.

The guy handed Joey the camera and posed with his wife and kids.

Can't Live without Them

When the Soviets had a problem, they knew where to turn.

Michael Sleppin of New York received an urgent letter from the largest circuit board facility in the Soviet Union.

"They had a technical problem," Sleppin said, "with the printed circuit board which is used in calculators and computers. I've been to Russia several times to help with certain problems. This time I solved it by writing back. I analyzed the problem and offered them alternatives."

Sleppin was amused when he received the letter for help. It came from a part of Russia from where his father emigrated at the turn of the century to escape pogroms.

He showed the letter to his father. "See, Dad, one day they throw us out, and next day they need us back."

Cheers in Hebrew

Lou Jacobi recalls doing *The Tenth Man* on Broadway in 1959. Paddy Chayefsky wrote it and Tyrone Guthrie directed. Everyone wondered how a Scots-Irishman could direct a Yiddish play based on the Dybbuk.

At the first rehearsal, the assembled cast consisted of Jack Gilford, George Voscovec, Rissa Schwartz (adopted daughter of Maurice Schwartz), and Jacobi.

Chayefsky refused to have any Yiddish or Hebrew in the play. "He wanted all dialogue to be purely English," Jacobi says. "We thought that was very strange for this particular Jewish play."

When Chayefsky walked out of the room, Guthrie asked, "What do you say when you clink glasses?" Everybody said *l'chaim.** Chayefsky came back and asked, "What's going on, Tony? I specified no Hebrew in the play."

Guthrie replied, "What would you have them say—cheers?"

Lou Jacobi

Front and Bach

Arthur Rubinstein once dropped into Café Society, where he was fascinated by busty pianist Hazel Scott.

"I knew you liked her boogie-woogie," said a friend, "but a great pianist like yourself—well, I didn't imagine you'd be so impressed with her Bach."

"Her Bach!" exclaimed Rubinstein. "It isn't her Bach, it's her front!"

---

* Literally "to life," customarily offered as a toast.

Two Is Cheaper

Abe Lebewohl

Abe Lebewohl, proprietor of the world-renowned Second Avenue Kosher Delicatessen, related that when one of his daughters was two years old, she became sick. He called the doctor, who was chief pediatrician at a hospital. Surprise! In those days they made house calls—at ten dollars!

"Let me check the other baby too," the doctor said. "For two, the price is fifteen dollars."

Message to America

Jane Fonda visited the Israeli troops on the front lines during the Lebanon campaign. In Jerusalem she asked the children for a message to bring back to the people of America.

"Tell them we want peace," one kid said.

"Tell them," another said, "we want all the Jews in America to come to Israel."

A third said, "Tell them we want *Dallas* here."

What Can I Tell You?

Roberta Wallach would make a poor guest on the tabloid television talk shows.

The daughter of Eli Wallach and Anne Jackson was invited on a *Phil Donahue Show* when the subject was children of famous parents. Naturally, everyone had a horror story to titillate the audience.

Then the host got to Roberta and she said, "What can I tell you? I love my parents!"

From left to right, Anne Jackson, Eli Wallach, and their daughters, Roberta and Katherine

What Competition?

In the late eighties, a rumor circulated that the world famed Louis Vuitton luggage company was engaging in discrimination and bias. The Anti-Defamation League (ADL) investigated and found that the charges were false.

"After we established the truth," national director Abraham Foxman said, "we felt it was our obligation to clear a name defamed. Truth and fairness are precious."

ADL officials brought the results of their investigation to the Louis Vuitton executives in Paris, where there was a great sigh of relief.

"Who spread those rumors?" the luggage makers asked.

"Possibly your competition," the ADL people said.

The Frenchmen were astonished: "Monsieur, Louis Vuitton has no competition."

Return of the Native

For someone who had strayed far from his roots, New York disc jockey Dave Herman suddenly found himself thrust into Jewish concerns and activity.

Herman was raised in an Orthodox milieu in the Bronx. He was the product of intensive religious upbringing, having come up through the grades at Salanter Yeshiva, Ramaz School, and the Talmudical Academy of Yeshiva University.

Then, as often happened even to kids with strict religious training, he made a 180-degree turn in his life. One of his teachers at Hunter College left to operate a radio station in Easton, Pennsylvania, and persuaded Dave to accompany him and begin a career as a disc jockey.

"When I went into radio," Dave says, "I went as far away from Judaism as you can get."

His first marriage, at age twenty-one, lasted seventeen years and produced two daughters.

Then he fell in love with a gentile woman, Libby Park.

Libby, a champion swimmer, began taking courses in Judaism. Dave went with her to classes at Ansche Chesed, a West Side synagogue that has attracted many professional people.

Libby took the next step and converted. Dave took his next step and married her. They have a son.

Dave is content with this twist in his life—another 180-degree turn, this time back to his roots. "I have returned to my heritage, culturally and spiritually."

At Least She's Still Joan

How did Joan Molinsky become Joan Rivers?

Her father, Dr. Meyer Molinsky, a surgeon, said that one day his daughter announced she wanted to be an entertainer. The father was adamantly opposed to the idea of his daughter in show business.

After a big argument, Joan ran away from home. Her father tracked her down to the YWCA on West Thirty-fourth Street. The register showed only one Joan, but it was a Joan Rivers. He brought her home, but the name stuck.

Joan Rivers

RICHARD GRANT & ASSOCIATES

Tripping Over Names

Songwriter Carol Connors, born Annette Kleinbard in New Brunswick, New Jersey, had two Academy Award nominations. She was nominated for her song *Someone's Waiting for You*, which she wrote for the Disney film *The Rescuers*. Her second nomination was for *Gonna Fly Now*, the theme song of Sylvester Stallone's first *Rocky* picture.

At the Academy Awards, Fred Astaire read the Best Song nominations and announced "Carol O'Connors." Her father turned to her and said, "Annettele, if you had used your name, Fred Astaire wouldn't have tripped over it."

"Daddy," she replied, "if I had used my name, Fred Astaire wouldn't have pronounced it."

Mama Knows Best

From right to left, Lorne Greene, Michael Landon, and Dan Blocker

Lorne Greene listened to his mother and became a superstar. It happened like this. In 1959 he made a pilot for *Bonanza*. Next day he called his mother in Florida. She told him that a friend of hers had died in Hollywood and asked him to go visit the home that night.

Lorne told Mom he'd be glad to go, but the next night. Well, you know mothers. When they want you to do something, it's that night. So Lorne went—that night.

He met an executive from NBC at the *shiva** house who liked the rough cut of *Bonanza*. Result? Lorne was signed to star in the new show. The series lasted fourteen years, was watched by 350 million fans in sixty-one countries, and made him a millionaire.

Moral of the story: Always listen to your mother.

All the Exercise He Needs

Prime Minister Shimon Peres visited Vice President George Bush at the White House. During a photo op, Bush told Peres about his tennis game. He asked whether Peres plays tennis. He said no. Bush asked whether he jogs or does any exercise. After all, Bush noted, the prime minister looks so fit. "I run the Israeli cabinet," Peres replied.

---

* "Seven" (Hebrew), referring to the seven days of mourning after interment.

Never Got the Money

Henny Youngman got his first job in vaudeville on Rosh Hashanah.

He had started out, fiddle in hand, making the rounds of agents, looking for any kind of booking. Finally he landed a job at the Sixteenth Street Theater in Brooklyn—for three dollars.

They neglected to tell Henny that the date fell on the High Holiday. The theater was located near the temple where he was supposed to be with his father that day.

"Right in the middle of my act," Henny relates, "my father and a cop stormed down the aisle and dragged me off the stage. I never got the three dollars."

Henny Youngman

Quick Thinking

Ron Shaw was not always a business executive (he runs the American office of the Japanese firm Pilot Pen Corporation). He started out at age eleven as a comedian.

Once he was emceeing at the Stage Coach Inn when Connie Francis was the headliner. He went out to introduce her: "Here she is, MGM's recording star . . ." Blank! He could not remember the name of the star.

"I faked a cough, turned around, and glanced at the music sheet with her name on it. I turned back quickly and announced her."

Best Day of His Life

Norm Crosby brought his wife and two sons to the dedication of his star on the Hollywood Walk of Fame. A reporter asked Andrew, who was eight at the time, how he felt about the ceremony. "It's one of the best days in my whole life," the kid said. "I didn't have to go to school today."

Norm Crosby

Big People, Lonely People

Goodman Ace, once the top name in radio with his popular *Easy Aces* on CBS, found out that big people are basically lonely people.

When he went to Hollywood as a writer, Doris Day, the biggest star at the time, invited him to dinner on a Saturday night at her palatial house. Ace expected to find the house full of people. Instead the huge table was set for two.

Doris was thrilled to have Goodman there. It was Saturday night, yet Goodman had no place to go and Doris had nothing to do. Can you imagine Doris Day lonely?

Sylvia Was a Shill for a Still

When jazz stylist Sylvia Syms was a six-month-old baby, the next door neighbor would offer to wheel her carriage outdoors. Of course Sylvia's mother was delighted to have someone care for the baby so she could get shopping and other errands done.

One day, as Sylvia's mother was shopping, she saw her baby's carriage standing unattended. Soon the kindly lady emerged from a doorway, pushed the carriage down the street, took something out of the carriage, and again disappeared into a building.

"Mother was puzzled," Sylvia related. "She went up to see what's going on. Seems our helpful neighbor was a bootlegger. She kept bottles of liquor in my carriage as she made her deliveries."

Power of Mezuzah

Sammy Davis, Jr., visited Eddie Cantor and admired a *mezuzah* on his makeup shelf. Eddie gave it to him. Sammy was thrilled, and wore it ever since.

After the automobile accident, when he lost an eye, Sammy was convalescing in a hospital in San Bernardino. Eddie came to visit and asked about the *mezuzah*.

"I wore the *mezuzah* night and day ever since you gave it to me," Sammy said. "The first time I failed to wear it was on the night of the accident, when I couldn't find it."

Being Observant Gets Him a Wife

Ron Rifkin

Pride of heritage proved of lifelong benefit to Ron Rifkin. He is not afraid to advertise his roots in public. In fact, that is how he met his wife.

Ron is a graduate of Yeshiva of Central Queens and had his bar mitzvah at Queens Jewish Center where he read the Torah and *davened Shacharit** and *Musaf.***

While understudying Joel Grey in *Come Blow Your Horn*, he brought a menorah backstage one Chanukah night. He invited all the Broadway actors to join in the candle lighting ceremony. From *Carnival* came a dancer named Ivy March.

Ron and Ivy have been married for thirty years.

Essential Element in the Experiment

Dr. Henry Heimlich, the creator of the Heimlich Maneuver, invented a device that could replace the esophagus. He was so proud that he arranged a demonstration to a group of colleagues.

"Eat this piece of bread, John," Heimlich instructed his patient.

"I can't eat," the patient replied.

Heimlich was devastated. The doctors looked at Heimlich, then at each other. Was something awry with his invention?

"Why can't you eat, John? You ate yesterday."

"They didn't bring down my teeth."

* Led the first part of the Sabbath morning service.
** Second part of the Sabbath morning service.

Secret of a Long Marriage

At his parents' sixty-fifth wedding anniversary, Alan King asked what kept them together through so many years.

"Hate!" his father said. "Hate kept us together. We wouldn't die. We wouldn't give each other the satisfaction."

Alan King with his wife, Jeanette.

TIM BOXER

Who Am I?

It was a changed Ali MacGraw who came back after a year and a half in Yugoslavia, where she filmed the *Winds of War* miniseries for ABC.

"All that time I was in a trance," she said. "I had participated in one of the most important things in my life."

She was so affected by Herman Wouk's stirring story of the Holocaust that she began questioning her own identity. For the first time in her life she asked, "Who am I?" (She was born in New York and raised an Episcopalian in Westchester.)

Her maternal grandfather, Maurice Klein, came from Budapest at fourteen and worked in a sweatshop in New York. "To me that says Jewish family."

These thoughts surfaced thirteen years after she portrayed Brenda Patinkin, the quintessential Jewish American Princess, in Philip Roth's *Goodbye Columbus*. (At first she was actually turned down for the part because it was said she was not a Jewish type.)

"It's disturbing," she said, "that here I am, a grownup, and have no idea who I am. Everybody who can tell me is dead."

DOUGLAS KIRKLAND

Ali MacGraw

Chicken Flicker on Kibbutz

Before she was the female lead in *The King of Comedy*, the Jerry Lewis-Robert De Niro film, Sandra Bernhard was a chicken flicker in Israel.

She was seventeen and just out of high school in Scottsdale, Arizona. She took a trip to Greece. The Yom Kippur War broke out and she went to do volunteer work on a kibbutz where they were shorthanded.

"I spent eight months cleaning chickens in the slaughterhouse at Kfar Menahem, near Rehovot. It was a growing up experience."

Sandra Bernhard

The Boss Walks

The only time Alan King appeared on Broadway was in 1965, in *The Impossible Years*.

During a tryout in New Haven, Connecticut, producer David Black was standing in front of the theater. He was quite shabbily dressed. A shoeshine boy asked, "Do you know Alan King?" Black said, "Sure, he works for me."

Just then a nattily dressed King came out of the theater and stepped into a chauffeured Rolls Royce and said, "Bye, Boss."

Learning from the Synagogue

Judy Garland

Judy Garland, who was not Jewish, said she owed "my voice quality, my tremolo, to singing at a synagogue as a kid."

In her autobiography, the actress June Allyson describes one of the many parties she and her husband, Dick Powell, hosted where the guests included Jack Benny, George Burns, and Judy Garland.

Powell and Burns had something in common–as kids both had formed singing groups. Burns had the Pee Wee Quartet and Powell had the Peter Pan Five.

Burns described how his group used to play at the ferry and catch pennies from the debarking passengers. Powell mentioned singing for the religious market—fifteen dollars from the Presbyterians on Sunday, ten dollars from the Episcopalians on Wednesday, and ten dollars from the Synagogue on Friday.

Judy Garland mentioned her debt to the synagogue: "My first agent didn't have the money to send me to a voice teacher so he sent me to the synagogue to copy what I heard and get emotion in my voice."

"Judy launched into an emotional Hebrew melody," Allyson writes, "and there was not a whisper as she sang."

What's a Nice Jewish Girl . . .

Blanche Baker went to Israel to star in a special Christmas television program titled *Joseph and Mary*. "Here was a nice Jewish girl playing the Virgin Mary," she said. "I met Menachem Begin and he said, 'I want to tell you how relieved I am that the part is in good hands.'"

Mike Todd and His Principles

"The events of my father's early life read like a Jewish Horatio Alger story." So begins Michael Todd, Jr.'s book *A Valuable Property*, about his colorful father. Emphasize "Jewish" and you have the measure of the man, for he always believed in the Jewish faith, no matter how far he strayed.

For instance, after his Broadway success in producing the musical *Up in Central Park*, he enlisted Arthur Kober, who was also Jewish, to adapt a series of short stories from the *New Yorker* about a Jewish family in the Bronx and the romantic ups and downs of the daughter. Elmer Rice was to direct the play, titled *Bella's Got a Fella*.

Todd rented a theater in Boston for the tryout and one in New York for the anticipated big Broadway premiere. Everything was proceeding smoothly. One day at rehearsals, Todd suddenly announced: "I know you fellows put a lot of work into this, but it comes out anti-Semitic and it's cheap. I'll give you back the rights, the set, and what I've invested in it for free."

Now that's a man—a man proud of who he is and what he stands for—even if it costs him.

From left to right, Mike Todd, Elizabeth Taylor, and Yul Brenner.

The Pictures Were Out of Sight

Elisa Loti

Elisa Loti, wife of playwright Joseph Stein (*Fiddler on the Roof, Zorba, Enter Laughing*), thinks often of her birthplace in Guayaquil, Ecuador. Her parents settled there after escaping from Nazi Germany. Her father was a doctor and president of the Zionist organization in Guayaquil; her mother was president of Women's International Zionist Organization (WIZO). Elisa's daughter Jennifer once took a trip to visit relatives there.

"She took a lot of pictures," Elisa said. "She took pictures of the house I was born in. It was very thrilling. But when she came back, none of the pictures came out."

Old Policy Revived

In the early 1980s, Israeli Deputy Minister of Foreign Affairs Yehuda Ben-Meir met a prominent United States senator at the King David Hotel in Jerusalem. The senator mentioned he had just come from Prime Minister Menachem Begin, from whom he had learned of a new policy.

"I'm not aware of any new policy," Ben-Meir said in surprise.

"Oh yes," the senator claimed. "The new policy is that you will pursue terrorists and destroy them."

"It's not a new policy," Ben-Meir said.

"No? How long have you had it?"

"For three thousand years."

Stay with the Original

When Barbra Streisand brought *Yentl* to the screen, she was asked on ABC's *20/20* why she never changed her name. Perhaps to Barbra Sands. It's better showbiz.

The only thing she had done about her name was to delete an "a" to make it unique. "I don't believe in changing things that you're given," she said. "Something is unnatural about it."

Barbra Streisand

Now Here's a Moral

Paul Sherman, who operated coat check concessions at such upscale *boîtes* as Basin Street East, El Morocco, and various luxury hotels, started out as a mail clerk at IBM. He was fourteen and made nine dollars a week.

One day the company's president asked him to fill his water glasses. The youngster got indignant at the order. After all, he was a mail clerk, not a waiter. So he quit.

"If I had stayed," Paul sighed, "who knows? I could be chairman of the board of IBM."

Moral: If the boss asks for water, bring it. Who knows, you might end up as a great company president—or a great waiter!

Case of the Missing Molars

Alexander Archer, a ninety-two-year-old photographer, was covering the annual dinner of Bnai Zion at the New York Hilton. He was staring at his chicken plate when he suddenly noticed something missing.

Then came an announcement from executive vice president Mel Parness: "A set of false teeth has been found. Whoever is missing it, please reclaim it at the dais."

No one came up.

Waiting for the Jew

Esterita "Cissy" Blumberg, whose father built the Green Acres Resort at Lake Huntington in the Catskills, told how New York Jews started buying farmland early in the century. They had to overcome latent anti-Semitism in the mountains. In fact, she said, there was a gentleman's agreement at Lake Huntington not to sell land to Jews.

Because Cissy's father had blue eyes and an English accent, he had no trouble closing a deal on eighty-seven acres. He arrived in town by rail and waited in the saloon for a ride to his property. A group of locals invited him to their table. He bought them a drink and told them a story. Then they bought him a drink and told him a story.

"Gentlemen," he asked, "what are you doing here?"

"We've come to meet the Jew," they laughed.

You can imagine how surprised they were to learn that their new drinking partner was Blumberg the Jew. The men, his new neighbors, rushed out to his property and quickly removed the oil-soaked rags from around the house.

Next, Food Stamps

Early in her playwriting career, Wendy Wasserstein was up for a Guggenheim fellowship. Her father, Morris, a textile manufacturer, asked, "What's that?"

"That," explained Wendy, "is a grant they give to artists to finish their work."

"No daughter of mine is going on welfare!" he exclaimed.

After Wendy received the $18,000 grant, she called her father: "Dad, I got welfare! Next year, food stamps!"

Wendy Wasserstein

Preparing for the Next Generation

Mike Todd, Jr., was living in Ireland with his second wife when she gave birth to their son. It was a difficult delivery; mother and child almost died.

Mike had a name picked for a girl, but not for a boy. So he called his uncle David Goldbogen in Lake Zurich, Illinois. His uncle was Mike Todd's brother and a religious Jew. He suggested the name David.

"I thought it was odd of my uncle, being Orthodox, to suggest that I name my baby David, the same name as his. Orthodox people don't name babies after living relatives.

"My son David was born on October 2. My uncle David died on October 6. Strange, it was as if he knew."

Named for Holocaust Relatives

Hollywood star Carroll Baker had a tempestuous marriage to theatrical director Jack Garfein. The union produced two lovely children but was severed after thirteen strife-torn years.

"One thing she did," Jack said, "that outweighed all the stupidities that came after was to name our daughter."

Carroll was twenty-three when their first baby was born; she insisted she be named "after your mother who was killed in Auschwitz."

Jack and Carroll attended the world premiere of her controversial movie, *Baby Doll*, and next day she gave birth to Blanche Joy Baker. Blanche is for Jack's mother; Joy is for his father's mother Freyda (Yiddish for "joy").

Jack is a survivor of several concentration camps. His father was murdered by the Nazis at Ordruf, a concentration camp in Germany.

The second child was a boy, and Jack told Carroll to name him after someone in her family. Again, much to her credit, she insisted that the newborn be named for Jack's martyred father. She asked what was his father's name, and Jack said Herman. She asked, "What did they call him?" and Jack said Hershel.

Their son, Hershel, grew up to become a classical composer. Blanche, of course, became an actress.

Taking One's Own Measure

Lou Jacobi says this is a true story. He was in the hospital. They wheeled in a little old man with a beard and skullcap. In the morning he wrapped black straps around his arm.

Another patient turned to Lou and remarked, "You got to give the Jews credit. First day in the hospital and already he can take his own blood pressure."

Lou Jacobi (right) with Oscar Brand.

The Press vs. Motherhood

When Lenore Hershey was the first female editor of *Ladies Home Journal*, she went to Simon and Garfunkel's first big concert at Lincoln Center. She sat behind Paul Simon's mother, who complained she could not get backstage to see her son.

"Like a bridge over troubled waters," Hershey said, "I gave her my business card and suggested she try again, identifying herself as me. It worked, proving that the press is more powerful than motherhood."

TIM BOXER

Totie Fields

Second Time for Both

Totie Fields and George Johnstone had been married twenty-seven years. She was born Sophie Feldman in Hartford, Connecticut. He was born a Methodist in Boston.

One night Totie woke up and declared, "You've got to convert, George."

"Right now?"

"No, before we die."

"Why?"

"I just realized, you can't be buried with me."

George converted in Beverly Hills. They married again, this time under the *chupah*,* in Las Vegas.

"You can't imagine," Totie related, "how strange it was to get married with your kids watching you."

Stiff-necked as Always

Alan King went to the bar mitzvah of his great-nephew's son at Kew Gardens Jewish Center in Queens. There were 180 people, and nobody liked the table they were seated at.

"Maybe that is why we survived through the diaspora," Alan said. "We listen to nobody. We are singularly independent. We do what we please. That's fine, but it plays havoc with the caterers!"

* Bridal canopy.

Sick of Each Other

Eddie Cantor and Al Jolson were appearing in competing shows in Chicago. "One morning," Cantor recalled in a book, *Sonny Boy: The World of Al Jolson*, "I came down with pleurisy and my doctor advised me to close my show and take a rest.

"I told the doc I can't because all the papers will say 'Jolson drives Cantor out of town.' Sick as I was, I kept going night after night. I got so weak I couldn't even walk out on stage, so I closed the show and left for New York.

"Imagine my amazement when I got off the train, picked up a New York paper and read that Jolson closed his show immediately after me. It turned out that he had been sicker than I, but kept going because he didn't want the newspapers to say 'Cantor drives Jolson out of town.'"

Eddie Cantor

A Bronx Challenge

It is 1955 in the South Bronx and the neighborhood bookies are watching the Jerry Lewis Telethon at Bernie Allen's Luncheonette. Bernie watched a lot of television because comedy jobs were scarce. He was an aspiring comedian. He would get a weekend booking at the Paddock and come home with a whopping thirty-five dollars for telling such gags as "I had a phone installed in my car, but had a rough time getting the booth in."

So he and his cronies are watching the tube when someone remarks, "Hey Bernie, why aren't you on the telethon with all the big shot comedians?"

What can Bernie say except, "I'll be on this afternoon."

Of course, they all knew better. As a matter of fact they bet twenty dollars.

Bernie slips outside, hops a cab, gets off at Carnegie Hall before a huge crowd. A guard lets nobody pass. You have to picture Bernie in a dirty T-shirt with BERNIE'S LUNCHEONETTE on it, and his soiled pants rolled up, like he really does not belong in front of Carnegie Hall. He sees his old

Bernie Allen and his daughter, Marilyn.

pal, cryin' comic Billy Vine, and walks past the guard arm in arm with Billy.

He spots a Marine bringing coffee to the stage. "I'm from the restaurant downstairs," Bernie says. "Let me give you a hand." And he takes the coffee. While Jerry Lewis and Dean Martin are busy on stage, Bernie pours coffee for each member of the band. But instead of pouring into a cup, he pours the coffee on the floor. Everybody breaks up.

Jerry walks over to see what's going on. Bernie explains that he is a comedian and has a twenty-dollar bet with the boys in the Bronx about being on the show. Jerry tells him not to make any jokes, just make a pitch for money, and places Bernie in front of the camera.

A lot of money was made that afternoon for the fight against muscular dystrophy—including twenty dollars for Bernie's pocket.

Halfway There

Driving from Boston to New York, Isaac Asimov and his wife finally caught sight of their destination. "Well, we're halfway there," he sighed.

"Half!" she said. "Why, there's the building."

"The other half," he said wearily, "is finding a parking place."

Isaac Asimov

Just in Time

Rabbi Emanuel Rackman was president of Bar-Ilan University when a woman called the university's newly opened adult institute.

"Up to what age do you accept students?" she asked.

"Up to 120 years," was the answer.

"Marvelous," the woman said. "I have 31 more years to go."

She signed up for a Hebrew poetry course, Rackman reports.

Crossroads in Life

Richard Rodgers once said that everybody faces a fork on the road of life. The genius composer came upon his own crossroads at age twenty-two, when prospects for success in the music business seemed pretty dim.

He and Larry Hart had written songs for about twenty-five amateur shows, but nobody cared for their music. They made little headway in professional Broadway circles. At the time, Rodgers lived with his parents (his father was a doctor), but he was thoroughly discouraged.

Richard Rodgers

He quit writing songs and took a job in the Garment Center for five dollars a week selling babies' underwear. He was promised a fine future: he would go out on the road peddling infants' underwear for five years, then take over the business.

Imagine—Richard Rodgers a babies' underwear tycoon!

"I was to let the man know the next day," Rodgers related years later. "Then the phone rang at dinner. It was Ben Kaye, my father's patient who did legal work for the Theater Guild."

Kaye wanted Rodgers to help with a show some kids were doing Sundays to buy tapestries for the Guild Theater. Rodgers and Hart decided to write the show. It resulted in *Garrick Gaieties* and it became a hit. "It put us on our feet," Rodgers said. "A year later I had three shows on Broadway."

The rest, as they say, is history. Rodgers became a titan of the musical theater, creating *Pal Joey, Carousel, South Pacific*, etc.

If Rodgers had not responded to that fateful phone call, which prompted him to make the most important choice in his life, he would not have given the world such songs as *Oh, What a Beautiful Morning, Nothing Like a Dame*, and *Hello Young Lovers*.

This Magazine's a Killer

When Zero Mostel was stricken during a tryout of *The Merchant* in Philadelphia, Sam Levene brought him chicken soup in the hospital. Also some art and men's magazines. Zero threw out the art magazines, saying they were old. He kept the racy men's magazines. While adjusting himself comfortably in bed, Zero fell on the floor and died. Levene cried, "I killed Zero."

Zero Mostel

UNITED PRESS INTERNATIONAL, INC.

Protecting His Interest

On his first trip to Israel, Eli Wallach went with his wife Anne Jackson and agent Peter Witte. In Bethlehem, a street vendor tried to sell him postcards. Eli declined, saying he would take his own pictures.

The vendor looked at Anne and said to Eli, "I will give you ten sheep and ten camels for her."

As Eli hesitated, Peter broke in: "Take it! I get ten percent!"

Eli Wallach and Anne Jackson

He Learns Fast

Israel's War of Independence gave birth to many stories of ingenuity, skill, and cleverness. One was related by Rabbi Joseph Grunblatt of Queens Jewish Center in New York.

A sergeant was demonstrating how to take apart a machine gun and reassemble it. He gave the weapon to a raw recruit and told him to do it.

"How are you doing?" he asked the eager young soldier.

"Fantastic!" he reported. "I even have a few pieces left over!"

They Came Through

CLEVELAND PRESS

When Chabad House burned down in Los Angeles, Jan Murray hosted a telethon to finance the rebuilding. But he told Rabbi Shlomo Cunin, head of the west coast Lubavitch, that he was worried about reaching the goal.

"Rabbi," he said, "we're not going to take in much money. We're on the air only four hours. Jerry Lewis was on for twenty-four hours and he brought in a million dollars."

"Don't worry," the rabbi said. "God took away and God will give back."

"It was amazing," Jan says. "In only four hours we raised $1,700,000 to rebuild the Chasidic center. When Jews get together, they really come out to help."

Jan Murray

What He Could Have Become

At twelve years of age, Herschel Bernardi auditioned for Sidney Kingsley and got the part. He ran home with the exciting news. "Ma, I got a Broadway job! They want you to come sign the contract."

Herschel Bernardi

His mother, wise to the ways of Broadway, said, "That's no job." Instead, they packed for Detroit, where Herschel did a whole season in a Yiddish play. That is security. On Broadway a show would be lucky to last through the night.

"The job I almost had," Herschel recalled years later, "was *Dead End*. I would have been one of the Dead End Kids. The guy who took my part was Bernard Punsley, who's now a successful orthodontist. See what I could have become?"

That reminded him of the man who wanted to be a *shammes*.* But he could neither read nor write, so the synagogue president turned him down. He went to work as a scrap iron peddler—and became a multimillionaire. One day they gave him an important paper to sign. He pushed it away. "If I could write, I'd be a *shammes*!"

Formula for Success

According to television producer Joe Cates, Gene Autry once asked Johnny Cash, "John, got any Jews working for you?"

"Maybe one," Cash said.

"If you want to get ahead," Autry said, "you better get some of them Jews working for you."

* Synagogue sexton.

Another One of Us

Gene Barry's wife, Betty, went to a shop on Fairfax Street to buy a *talit* for their son's bar mitzvah. The owner looked at the check and asked, "Are you the wife of Gene Barry?" She said yes. He was so surprised he ran upstairs and shouted to his wife, "Bat Masterson is Jewish!"

Betty and Gene Barry

Stork Wins the Race

Robert Merrill was not present at the birth of his son forty years ago. At the time he was starring in the Metropolitan Opera's *Barber of Seville* in Cleveland.

"I had an open telephone in the wings direct to Doctors Hospital in New York," he related. "Between acts I'd come off stage and talk to Marion's mother, who was at her bedside. Marion was due any minute.

"At the end of the show she hadn't delivered yet. I got on the next plane to New York, where a limousine was waiting for me. When I rushed into the hospital, Marion's mother grabbed my arm and pulled me over to a window. There was my son. David was born twenty minutes ago, while I was in the limo. He looked like a raisin. Now he's a rock singer."

Bea Arthur   Gene Saks

Typical Hollywood

Director Gene Saks was married to Bea Arthur for twenty-nine years before they divorced.

"It lasted so long," I said, "It certainly wasn't your typical Hollywood marriage."

"No," he said, "but it broke up in Hollywood."

So Far It Has Lasted

Adrianne Tolsch dated Bill Scheft seven years before deciding to marry. She hopes the marriage will last longer than her first one.

"I was divorced before the wedding pictures were developed—and they were Polaroids!"

Got It Coming to Her

Albert Hague, an acting coach to many Hollywood stars and who played the music teacher in both the movie and TV series *Fame*, was born in Berlin. His father was a psychiatrist and his mother a champion chess player. His father died in 1930, leaving a pension to his widow. Three years later the Nazis stopped payment.

In the fifties, while the widow Mimi Martin worked as a dietitian at a Jewish hospital in Brooklyn, she sued the German government to restore the pension. Albert called to break the good news that she won her case.

"That's nice," she said.

"Is that all you can say?"

"Why should I get excited? It's my money."

Price Is Right

David Ben-Gurion, according to Molly Picon, attended the ceremonies when the Kaiser-Fraser plant rolled off its first Israeli-assembled automobile. They were going to present him with their first car.

Since government officials are forbidden to accept gifts, the prime minister was going to give them a one-pound note. As the shiny new car rolled off the assembly line, Ben-Gurion reached into his pocket. He turned to his wife.

"Paula, what should I do? I only have a two-pound note."

"David, at this price, take two."

Nothing Can Move Him

Eddie Fisher

Eddie Fisher says he lost Grossinger's because of a false report in a supermarket tabloid. The story was that his son Todd, a born-again Christian, had converted his father.

"It wasn't true, of course," Eddie says.

Because of that erroneous article, Eddie claims Grossinger's, which had been his second home, stopped booking him.

Eddie admits that Todd tried to influence him, but he resisted. He says he is Anschel Yankel, a proud and steadfast Jew.

Smuggling a Life to Safety

If it wasn't for his brother shlepping him inside a sack toward Buchenwald, Yisroel Meir Lau would not be the chief rabbi of Israel today. Heck, he wouldn't be alive!

The Nazis took the Polish *shtetl** of Piotrekow and rounded up all the Jews. Naphtali, at fifteen, was put with a group of young people to be taken for slave labor in Buchenwald. His father, the local rebbe, was shipped out with all the older men to the Treblinka death factory. Naphtali's four-year-old brother Yisroel was doomed to accompany his mother and the rest of the women to perish in the slave labor camp of Ravensbruck.

Mother pushed the child away from her. Naphtali deftly scooped him up and stashed him in his duffel bag. He carried the little boy in the bag over his shoulders all the way to Buchenwald.

A life was saved by being smuggled into a concentration camp!

---

* Small town, particularly in the Jewish communities of Eastern Europe.

Too Early

Ezer Weizman went with his attorney, Leon Charney, to meet with former President Jimmy Carter in Atlanta.

Leon had *yahrzeit** for his father, Morris Charney, so he got up early for services at Congregation Beth Jacob. Weizman and Robert Lipshutz, Carter's former presidential counsel and now an Atlanta attorney, accompanied Leon to the six-thirty *minyan*.

"The only time I got up so early," Weizman quipped, "was to go to war."

Ezer Weizman

Learning to Act Jewish

Rod Steiger, whom some people think is Jewish, probably because of the tremendous impact he made with his realistic portrayal of the Holocaust survivor in *The Pawnbroker*, was born Lutheran and is agnostic.

To prepare for his role as the Satmar rebbe in *The Chosen*, he said he "picked up the Jewish accent in a butcher shop on Sixth Avenue. I listened to the butcher talking to two women. I also went to services in Crown Heights, Brooklyn, where I saw the great Lubavitch leader, Rabbi Schneerson."

Steiger also pulled on his background for inspiration. "I grew up in Newark, crossroads of a million housing projects. I was the only Gentile in a Jewish neighborhood. I was six years old and used to light the oven for a Jewish woman every Friday night. I was a Shabbes goy."

---

* Anniversary of a death, observed by the lighting of the memorial lamp for twenty-four hours and reciting the *Kaddish* prayer at services.

The Power of Klezmer

Giora Feidman

Giora Feidman is one of the world's renowned klezmer players. His father, grandfather, and great-grandfather were all klezmers. Klezmer, he notes, is derived from the Hebrew— *kley* (instrument) and *zemer* (song).

"For thousands of years," he says, "Jews have communicated with God through music. Jewish music is one of the highest expressions of humanity. You don't say a prayer, you sing a prayer."

To show how klezmer reaches the soul of a Jew, he related how he performed for the Israeli wounded during the 1967 Six-Day War.

"In one bed was a soldier who was burned, dehydrated, his face blackened. He didn't utter a word. After I played, we heard him sigh.

"A nurse said, 'For ten days I haven't heard a sound from him. Now I understand the power of the klezmer.'"

So There!

Jews have been disproportionately represented in the world of chess. For fifty-five years, until 1921, the world chess champions were two Jews, Wilhelm Steinitz, a German, and Emanuel Lasker, an American.

Steinitz was once baited by an anti-Semitic opponent, Johannes von Zukertort, who said, "You are not a chessplayer, but a Jew."

The champ retorted, "You, apparently, are neither."

In His Father's Footsteps

Zero Mostel's son, Josh, decided to pursue an acting career, just like his talented father. When Josh started out with The Proposition, an improvisational group, his illustrious father sent a telegram: "If you want to follow in your father's footsteps, use Desenex."

Josh Mostel

The Day Time Stood Still

Arne Melchior, scion of a distinguished Jewish family in Denmark, remembers when he was a member of the Danish delegation to the United Nations—and almost fell asleep.

He had to sit through the boring, interminable speeches of Baroodi, the Saudi Arabian ambassador.

One day Baroodi began his speech at eleven o'clock in the morning. He spoke and spoke, on and on. Suddenly at one o'clock he stopped.

The assembly president picked up his head and inquired ever so tactfully, "May I ask the distinguished gentleman from Saudi Arabia if he finished his speech?"

"No, I am not!" Baroodi snapped. "I only looked at my watch and I see I have plenty of time."

Melchior whispered to the Danish ambassador, "Better he should have looked at the calendar."

Credit Amex for Holocaust Flick

DAVID JAMES

On location in Poland, Steven Spielberg (left) directs Schindler's List, starring Liam Neeson (right) as Oskar Schindler.

If American Express had not been so slow in verifying a credit card purchase, *Schindler's List* might never have been written or filmed.

Thomas Keneally, an Australian author, was at a Beverly Hills hotel autographing copies of his new book, *The Confederates*. His writing hand ached for a break, so he picked up his well-worn briefcase and strode out for a walk. He peered at a luggage store where the window display of luxurious leather items drew him in. He really did not need a new bag, but he could not resist replacing the dilapidated one which had served him so well for so long.

Leopold Page, the heavily accented proprietor, gave him an offer he could not refuse. Keneally handed over a credit card. Page tried to verify the card. Inexplicably it took forty-five minutes for the transaction.

During this long wait, Keneally mentioned that he was signing his bestseller around the corner. Page was duly impressed.

"I have a story for you," Page said.

"Everybody wants to sell me a story. I have my own story."

"What is your story?"

"You see, I was supposed to be a priest. Two weeks before ordination my mother became sick. I took her to a Catholic hospital. I met a gorgeous nun and we fell in love. I asked for dispensation from the pope. We married and have two beautiful girls."

"That is a wonderful story," Page said. "I have a story, not about me, but about a German, Catholic, drinker, womanizer, member of army intelligence, He was in Cracow from 1939 to 1945 and tried to save Jews, starting with fifteen and ending up with 1,316 people designated to die."

"You know, Mr. Page, I am not the man to write the story."

"Give me three good reasons why not."

"I was three years old when the war started, my school taught us very little about this period, and besides, I know nothing about Jewish suffering."

"Mr. Keneally, you just gave me three good reasons to write the book. You know nothing about the Holocaust. I was a professor in Poland and I will teach you. I was in the Holocaust for five and a half years. I will tell you what happened day by day.

"You say you know nothing about Jewish suffering. Irish people suffered for four hundred years. Jews suffered for two thousand years. Jewish suffering and Irish suffering are the same. They suffer the same way."

By the time American Express decided that Keneally's credit was indeed valid, the deal was done. Keneally bought a new briefcase at a terrific discount, and left Page's shop to write the book which was published in 1982. However, it took ten more years for the film to be made by Steven Spielberg.

Page is happy that the story has finally been told, for he was one of the people on that list.

Who Else Would Buy This?

Molly Picon lived for thirty years in a sprawling house on twelve acres in Mahopac, New York.

She said her husband, Jacob Kalich, named it *Chez Shmendrik*.

"Yonkel said you have to be a *shmendrik** to put so much money in the ground."

Molly Picon

TIM BOXER

* An inept person, a nincompoop.

It's the Jewish Thing to Do

SIDNEY GLUCK

Bel Kaufman

Bel Kaufman, granddaughter of Sholom Aleichem and author of *Up the Down Staircase*, reveals that the world almost never got *Fiddler on the Roof*.

Sheldon Harnick was prepared to write the lyrics for a musical based on Tevye the milkman. He tried several times to call Sholom Aleichem's family lawyer to negotiate the rights to the Tevye stories, but could never reach him.

When Bel found out that the lawyer was unreachable, she was appalled. "Why do we keep such an incompetent lawyer?" she asked.

Her aunt gave a very Jewish answer: "Bellachke, we have to keep him. He's a very sick man."

Jewish Is Better

Six-year-old Peter asked, "Mom, are you Jewish?"

"No, son," Arlene Francis said.

"Is dad Jewish?"

"Yes," she said about Martin Gabel. "But that doesn't mean anyone is better than the other."

"Yes it does," Peter said. "If you're Jewish, you wouldn't have to work today—it's Yom Kippur."

Time to Rhyme

New York's Lieutenant Governor Betsy McCaughey and her new husband, Wilbur Ross, came to honor Abe Hirschfeld. Abe was celebrating his second seventy-fifth birthday at a 1995 Chanukah party sponsored by Minyan of the Stars. (He marked his first seventy-fifth birthday the previous year.)

Minyan of the Stars is a nonprofit organization created by Joseph Papp to enable people in show business to rediscover their Jewish heritage and reaffirm their Jewish identity by observing the holidays throughout the year.

From left to right, Abe and Zipora Hirschfeld with Betsy and Wilbur Ross.

ROBERT KALFUS

Betsy and Wilbur recited a poem in Abe's honor which ended:

> We shall treasure this event
> It truly is from heaven sent.
> We always wondered from afar
> How does a Minyan have a Star?
> Now we've seen this awesome show
> And we've learned how minyans grow.

Calling the Almighty

TIM BOXER

Menachem Begin

Shmuel Moyal, press representative of the Israeli Mission to the United Nations, relates that Menachem Begin tried to telephone Ronald Reagan for hours, but no answer. Finally the president picked up the phone and apologized: "I've been busy, Menachem. I've been talking to God. I have a long distance line to him."

Next day Reagan tried in vain to reach Begin. When Begin at last answered, he said, "I'm sorry Ronnie, but I, too, have been talking to God—only in Jerusalem it's a local call."

Face the Facts

Sammy Davis, Jr., was in the lobby of the Concord Resort Hotel on his way to the golf course when a woman asked, "Are you really Sammy Davis?"

"With this *punim** who could I be?" he said.

"I didn't recognize you," she said. "You didn't have your jewelry on."

Not to Be Outdone

Shmuel Moyal, press representative of the Israel Mission to the United Nations, tells of the time John F. Kennedy said proudly that he is president of two hundred million people. Whereupon David Ben-Gurion replied, "I'm prime minister of three million prime ministers."

* Face.

Now That's a Deal

Monty Hall is well known in Hollywood as a most charitable person. Some call him Mr. *Tzedaka** for all the benefits and fund-raising he does for Variety Clubs as well as Israel Bonds, United Jewish Appeal, Hadassah, and every disease out there. He has a garage full of plaques and citations from every organization imaginable. He has done benefits at so many hotels that the waiters think he is the maitre d'.

Monty Hall

He says he lives like Tevye—by tradition, the tradition of *tzedaka.*

Charity was part of his family life in Winnipeg. His mother, Rose Halparin, was once head of Hadassah there. Monty himself was the recipient of charity in his youth and, as a result, he has been paying back ever since.

After completing high school, he became a delivery boy. A wealthy man who saw Monty in the street asked his father why the boy was not in college. The father said he could not afford tuition.

The man made a deal with Monty. He would advance the money for a college education provided Monty maintained high marks, repaid the loan, and later helped other kids in need.

That was Monty's first deal.

He graduated from University of Manitoba, became a disc jockey in Toronto, and achieved fabulous success as host of *Let's Make a Deal* on television. He paid back that loan, and continued to repay with countless acts of *tzedaka*, setting a paramount example for other Hollywood personalities.

---

* Literally "justice," connoting philanthropy, charity, benevolence.

Kaddish for Mamaleh*

Mitchell Parish

Songwriter Mitchell Parish, who wrote such standards as *Sweet Lorraine, Sophisticated Lady, All My Love, Let Me Love You Tonight, Volare,* and *Stars Fell on Alabama,* among many others, visited his mother Rona in the hospital as she lay dying.

"I want someone to say *Kaddish* for me," she said, "even if you have to pay someone to do it."

Mitchell made a promise: "I'm going to say it. No one is going to say it for me."

The man who wrote *Mamaleh,* which Jan Peerce recorded, went to New York's Actors Temple morning and night for eleven months to say *Kaddish* for his *mamaleh.*

The Ultimate Gig in Show Biz

Joey Bishop was sixty-three before he made his Broadway debut. He filled in for Mickey Rooney for several weeks, costarring with Ann Miller in the smash musical *Sugar Babies.*

He decided to make his appearance on the Great White Way because he did not want to disappoint his two little grandsons. He feared that when they were older they would ask, "What did you do in show business?" He would say he made movies, was on television, worked the night clubs.

They would say, "Were you ever on Broadway?"

"If I said no," Joey sighed, "they'd stop talking to me."

---

* Mother, a term of endearment.

Collecting for Trees

Jerry Lewis says that the Jewish National Fund (JNF) played a role in his life. As a youngster, he'd run with the other kids to place the blue-and-white boxes in homes and collect the money to plant trees in Israel.

So it was not inappropriate for him to serve as toastmaster at a JNF dinner in honor of *Parade* editor Walter Anderson.

However, the question that bothered Jerry was: "Why this gentile? There are so many Jews in New York who would love this honor."

Jerry Lewis

A Page in the Book

Poldek Pfefferberg, who survived the Holocaust as one of Oskar Schindler's Jews, came to the United States in 1947. A former Polish professor, he could speak Russian, German, Yiddish, and Polish, but very little English.

The naturalization clerk did not fancy Poldek Pfefferberg. It sounded too German.

"You should change it now," the clerk said, "because later it will cost you five hundred dollars."

She opened the telephone book and turned the pages.

"Look under P," the immigrant said, "at least leave me my initial."

She named him Leopold Page.

"I didn't know it meant a page in the book," he says now. "I would have changed for something better."

She Has No Problem with That

Rabbi Joseph Potasnik of Congregation Mount Sinai in Brooklyn Heights, while officiating at the funeral of Louis Heller, a well-known Brooklyn matrimonial judge, recalled the time a young Heller was walking with his mother on Fifth Avenue. They went into a store where *The Jewish Hour* was being broadcast. During a break the mother was asked, "Would you mind sampling this gefilte fish?"

"I have no problem with that," she said and tasted the fish.

"What do you think?"

"My grandmother couldn't make fish as good as this."

"Would you mind saying that on the air?"

"I have no problem with that."

She again sampled the fish and said, "My grandmother couldn't make fish as good as this and, by the way, if you need a good lawyer, my son Louie just graduated from Brooklyn Law School."

Heller was aghast. In those years it was illegal for lawyers to advertise on radio.

"Ma, you can't say that!" he cried.

"Why not, Louie? About the gefilte fish I was lying. About you I was telling the truth."

Finally Home

United States Secretary of State George Schultz did his best to help prisoners of conscience in the Soviet Union. He recalls participating in a 1987 Passover *Seder* in Moscow with refuseniks Ida Nudel, Josef Begun, and Vladimir Slepak, among others.

He says the high point in his career came when he received a phone call from Jerusalem. Ida Nudel was on the line.

"Where are you?" he asked.

"I am home," she answered.

Ida Nudel

The Pintele Yid*

Jane Seymour, who played the role of Natalie Jastrow in Herman Wouk's television miniseries, *War and Remembrance*, read the script and was "totally destroyed emotionally. I found myself weeping on the pages."

The role went a lot deeper for the actress, who was born Joyce Frankenberg in England to a Polish-Jewish physician, John Frankenberg, who had escaped from Nazi Germany with his Dutch wife.

For her role, she had to learn Hebrew and Yiddish and how to make the blessing over the Shabbes candles. She also had to learn a nursery song, *Rozhinkes mit Mandlen*.

Jane Seymour

She called her father and sang the Yiddish tune on the phone. "He burst into tears," she recalls. "He said the last time he heard it was when his grandmother sang it to him.

"I felt a sudden enormous pride for a people that were being very efficiently destroyed. Not having any religious base myself—and my father not even a believer and my mother not Jewish—and never having thought of having any sort of Jewish blood, I felt enormous pride at being in this film.

"I think for the first time I felt . . . Jewish."

---

* Assimilated Jew who nevertheless harbors a faint feeling for his heritage.

Building Bridges to Peace

Ambassador Colette Avital, Consul General of Israel in New York, said that Yitzhak Rabin left Israel in the 1950s to study at the Royal Military Academy in England. Although the Arab students did not fraternize with the Israelis, Rabin made friends with an Arab officer named Maher.

Years later, after Prime Minister Rabin signed a peace treaty with Jordan's King Hussein, he visited Amman. His old friend Maher was waiting for him at the airport.

Yitzhak Rabin and Nina Boxer.

Soon after, Maher suffered a stroke. Magen David Adom dispatched an ambulance over the border to rush him to Hadassah Hospital in Jerusalem. Rabin was waiting for him at the hospital.

"That was how Rabin made peace—by building bridges between people," Avital said.

Almost a Desecration

When the CBS-TV film *The Attic: The Hiding of Anne Frank* was being shot in Amsterdam, the producers ran into a great deal of antagonism from the Dutch.

"The Dutch were one of the few people who had stood up to the Nazis," said executive producer Michael Lepiner. "To see those Nazi flags on the buildings again, and Nazi troops in the street, was almost a desecration. People broke into tears."

Abe Foxman

Return to Yiddishkeit*

Each year the High Holy Days conjure up conflicting images of the cross and Magen David for Abe Foxman, national director of the Anti-Defamation League.

It was during this New Year's season in 1945 when he first became aware he was actually Avraham and not Henryk, the little Catholic boy who spent the Holocaust years reared on the catechism of the church.

After the war, his father, Joseph, who survived the Vilna ghetto, reclaimed his son from the nanny. She had adopted the boy and had him baptized. The elder Foxman wondered how to "reconvert" his son and bring him back to Yiddishkeit.

It was Simchat Torah, when Jews rejoice over the cyclical reading of the Five Books of Moses. The father took Avraham by the hand and together they walked to the Great Shul of Vilna.

On the way they passed a church. The child crossed himself, just as he was taught.

They passed a priest. The child dropped his father's hand, took the priest's hand and kissed it, just as he was taught.

"The celebration in *shul*," Foxman recalls, "was a mixture of anguish and joy. This was the *shearith haplaytah*.** These survivors of Auschwitz had made their way back to Vilna and were now celebrating life and Yiddishkeit."

Avraham told his father that he liked "the Jewish church" much better than the Catholic church because "there was singing and dancing and happiness."

* Jewish tradition.
** Survivors.

A Soviet Army officer spotted the young boy and asked the father, "Is he Jewish?"

Told he was, the officer's eyes clouded. "I've traveled thousands of kilometers the last four years and have not been able to find a Jewish child alive." He hoisted the boy on his shoulders and cried, "This is my *Sefer Torah*,*" and danced with a heart of joy and eyes of tears.

"This was my first conscious feeling of being a Jew," Foxman says.

Inspiration from Parents

Robert Lippet, president of the Sheet Music Society and an expert on movie lore, tells about lyricist Sheldon Harnick's problem in fixing a troubled *Fiddler on the Roof* prior to its Broadway opening.

He labored three days and came up with a new song, *Do You Love Me?*

"Sheldon walked out of the theater in tears," Lippet says. "He remembered that his parents had an unhappy marriage. He realized that the song he wrote was about the relationship he wished his mother and father had had."

Robert Lippet

Who Needs It?

Marilyn Michaels bought four apartments on the West Side and made one big mansion-sized home. She says she now has four kitchens "but I don't use any. One is a closet, one is an office, one is a laundry room."

"What's the main kitchen?" I asked.

"That's the order-up room."

---

* Scroll of Law, the Torah.

*Cantor Joseph Malovany
(left) and Donald Trump.*

Kosher Is an Art

Joseph Malovany, the world-famed cantor of Fifth Avenue Synagogue, went to Poland to do a concert. He had marked his luggage with his name, and the authorities refused to release it.

"Malovany means artist in Polish," he said. "They thought I was smuggling paintings. They opened my bags and all they found was frozen kosher food."

She Saw It Coming

When the Germans came to the little Romanian town of Sighet and began rounding up the Jews, Elie Wiesel's wise old grandmother was the only one who had a premonition.

He remembers her as a simple, beautiful, pious woman with a black kerchief. Every Friday, when he returned from *cheder*,* she would greet little Elie with a piece of delicious warm homebaked *challah*.** "She just wanted to hear me say *Hamotzi*."***

As they were herded to the trains, the Jews believed they would come back some day soon. "My grandmother knew we wouldn't," Elie says. "She boarded the train with her *tachrichim***** on."

---

*   Hebrew School.
**   Bread, especially baked for the Sabbath.
***   Blessing before eating bread.
**** Burial shrouds of white linen.

Finding Yourself

A twenty-two-year-old Jewish man desperately trying to find himself left the comfort of his home in Spring Valley, New York, to seek spiritual balm in a land far away.

According to Rabbi Michael Alony, who revealed the details at the Concord Resort Hotel, the son stormed out of the house after a bitter family fight, vowing that his father would never see him again.

He took his Catholic girlfriend and traveled to Katmandu, in the mountains of Nepal, to find himself. The young man and his girlfriend became disciples of a guru for six years.

One day a friend from home arrived. "I'm sorry about the bad news," he said.

"What bad news?"

"Didn't you know? Your father died of a massive coronary three months ago."

The son was devastated, overwhelmed with guilt. Feeling responsible for his father's death, he went off again in search of himself. He longed to go to Israel, but was afraid of alienating his gentile girlfriend. They first visited Jordan and Egypt.

"We're so close," he said. "Let's go see what it's like in Israel."

They made their way to the Western Wall. There he was able to let go of his suppressed emotions in a *kvitl:** "Dear father, forgive me for causing you pain and grief—and for killing you."

Eyes clouded with tears, the young man groped for an empty crack in the Wall to insert his precious piece of paper. He dislodged someone else's note. It fell to the ground.

---

* A note slipped into the cracks of the Western Wall on which a petition has been inscribed.

He opened it and read: "Dear Howie, If you ever come to the Western Wall, you should know that you didn't kill me. Have no regrets. I love you."

It was signed by his father and had his Spring Valley address.

Howie did not know what to make of it. He wanted to stay in the Holy City another day. His young girlfriend, however, wanted to return to their new home in Katmandu. So they came to a parting of the ways.

It was Friday night. Howie was alone at the *Kotel*.* He prayed. A rabbi from Aish Hatorah invited him to experience Shabbat with two dozen other young people at his home.

Howie spent the next four years studying at Aish Hatorah Yeshiva. He was now thirty-two, with full beard and *peyot*.** His rabbi said it was time to think of getting a wife. A matchmaker determined his likes and interests, then arranged a meeting with a compatible young lady.

It was his Catholic girlfriend!

When she broke off with Howie four years prior, she changed her mind about going back to the guru. She stayed in Jerusalem, where she became a student at the yeshiva of Rabbi David Revson. She converted and was now an observant Jew.

Howie finally found himself. But not in Katmandu.

It was Jerusalem that opened his eyes. His search for self-revelation led him back to his girlfriend. She was waiting to join him once again on a quest—only this time under the *chupah*!

---

* The Western Wall.
** Sidelocks, worn particularly by Hasidim.

A Change of Heart in Mitn Drinnen*

Jewelry designer Aya Azrielant asked her firstborn, five-year-old Jonathan, if he would like a baby brother or sister. Jonathan said it was a good idea to have a sibling.

When Aya was eight months pregnant, Jonathan told her, "I gave it a lot of thought and I decided we should cancel it."

Ofer and Aya Azrielant

You Are What You Are

After Joey Bishop became a huge comedy star, he went back to Philadelphia to work in a club.

"I don't know if it's so good to be appearing in your hometown," he said. "You work for years to achieve stardom. Then you walk down the street and someone yells, 'Hey, it's Joey Gottlieb.'"

* Suddenly.

Knowing When You're Alive

Gershon Kekst

Gershon Kekst, head of a financial communications firm, was guest of honor at an American Committee for the Weizmann Institute of Science benefit. He recalled what Weizmann president Chaim Harari once told him: "If you're past fifty and wake up in the morning with no aches and pains, you should go back to bed because you are probably dead."

The Shtetl as Illusion

Miriam Margolyes went to Czechoslovakia for a part in Barbra Streisand's film *Yentl.* To recreate the *shtetl* population, fifty seniors from the remaining Jews in Prague were bused to the countryside two hours away.

"They stood in the middle of this invented *shtetl*," Miriam recalls, "and gazed in wonder at this place which represented their own homes that had been destroyed in the Holocaust.

"Slowly they walked around to the back of the buildings and found— nothing. They were shocked to see their beloved *shtetl* was nothing but a movie set.

"It was so painful to see their disappointed faces when they realized their real world was gone and they were now in a pretend world."

We Talk to Think

Don't underestimate the power of words, said Bard College president Leon Botstein at the seventieth annual dinner of YIVO* Institute for Jewish Research at The Plaza in New York.

Botstein, whose father came from Lodz, Poland, reflected on the difference between Christian and Jewish schools.

"In the Christian school they say, 'Don't raise your hand until you know what you think.'

"In the Jewish school," Botstein said, "I raise my hand because I want to think. I talk in order to learn."

Wall of Fame in Proper Frame

Eighty show business portraits make up the Jewish Celebrity Wall of Fame on display at Broadway's Jerusalem II Restaurant. But there are four celebrities you ought not to invite to view this photo exhibit.

Owner Eddie Fishbaum, whose restaurant is certified kosher by the Orthodox Union, took four pictures off the wall lest they offend the sensitivities of his strictly Orthodox patrons.

He removed Sarah Jessica Parker and Carol Kane because religious customers might be offended by the actresses' bare arms.

Claire Barry's photo was similarly banned because she showed a slight hint of cleavage. Lainie Kazan's photo was rejected because her lips formed a kiss aimed at the photographer—me!

* Yidisher Visenshaftlikher Institut, Institute for Jewish Research.

It's How You Were Brought Up

Growing up Jewish meant different things to different people. To Richard Lewis, it meant the world revolved around eating. "You're not sick," his mother would say. "You're just hungry."

The day Tovah Feldshuh announced her intention to become an actress, Grandma Ada responded, "Why don't you just go into the kitchen and get a challah knife and stick it in my heart now?"

When David Brenner went swimming in the ocean, his mother made him wear rubber wingtip shoes and a red bathing suit (it used to be his sister's—he had to roll it down). "I went to the beach infrequently," he said, "because I had to wait three weeks after eating lunch."

Kvelling in Church

Film producer Rob Fried, who earned an Academy Award for *Session Man*, was filming another movie in San Francisco when his mother and father came to visit. The movie was *I Married an Axe Murderer*, starring Alan Arkin and Amanda Plummer.

Naturally he put his parents to work as extras in a church scene.

"We sit in the front pew and are *kvelling*,*" Sally Fried said. "How's that for *nachas*?**"

* To swell with pride.
** Satisfaction from another's achievement.

They Love Bagels, or Do They?

Who else could write an endearing book about bagels but Marilyn and Tom Bagel? Their *Bagel Bible* is a fascinating guide to great noshing. They even got some of their favorite celebrities to expound on their love of bagels.

"Why do I like bagels?" Joan Rivers says. "They seem to like me. They go right to my thighs and won't leave."

Bob Hope eats only one bagel a year. "I prefer to eat donuts before they're soaked in cement."

Phyllis Diller warns never to eat day-old bagels. "There is a day-old bagel someplace in this world with teeth in it—mine."

Bob Hope

First You Speak, Then You Listen

Dr. Charles Kelman, the noted ophthalmologist, told the Nassau Region of Hadassah about the first time he gave a lecture.

There was but one person in the audience. Kelman proceeded with his slides and lecture for an hour, then started packing up.

"Dr. Kelman," the lone listener said, "you can't leave yet."

"Why not?"

"I'm the next speaker."

Shading History to Open a Door

Abba Eban recalled the time just before statehood when David Ben-Gurion was seeking arms for what he knew would be an inevitable war with the neighboring Arab states.

"We tried desperately to meet with Harry Truman," Eban said. "But he had no time or patience with us. He was busy fighting what in his eyes was the greatest of all enemies after the Soviet Union—the Republicans in Congress."

Eban said he had to secure a meeting for Chaim Weizmann with the president. Weizmann had no jurisdiction or authority, but was the only Zionist Truman might agree to meet. But the president's irascibility against what he called "Jewish pressure" was so intense that he refused to see him.

The next best chance was to work through Truman's former Kansas City business partner, Eddie Jacobson. Truman threw Eddie out, shouting, "You bald-headed S.O.B.! Don't worry me with

Abba Eban (center) with President Harry S Truman and Dr. Vera Weizmann.

all that pressure!" (Incidentally, the president had no compunction in spelling out S.O.B.)

Persuading Truman that Weizmann was the parallel in Jewish history of the great president from Missouri, Andrew Jackson, was the next approach. Eddie went back to the White House, pointed to a statue of Jackson, and boldly announced, "Chaim Weizmann is the Andrew Jackson of the Jewish people."

Truman responded with characteristic elegance: "All right, you S.O.B., get him in here."

"Now," Eban said, "my own view as a student of world history is that no two people ever walked on the surface of the earth with fewer common attributes than Andrew Jackson and Chaim Weizmann. But if that was necessary to get Weizmann in, it seemed to me that the establishment of Jewish statehood was of superior interest to historical truth."

It's All Relative

After Mexican President Carlos Salinas de Gortari received the 1992 World Statesman Award from Rabbi Arthur Schneier's Appeal of Conscience Foundation, he related a recent exchange with Jacob Frenkel, governor of the Bank of Israel.

Salinas, whose government had just renewed ties with the Vatican after a 130-year lapse, said his country was often called "Poor Mexico—so far from God, so close to the United States."

Frenkel told him what they say about his country: "Poor Israel—so close to God, so far from the United States."

Kissing His Own Mezuzah

Harry Wittlin

Harry Wittlin, owner of the Pickwick Arms Hotel on the East Side, lives in a luxury building. One day he noticed that his Jewish neighbor did not have a *mezuzah* on his apartment door. Harry had an extra one, so he affixed it to his neighbor's door.

Next day Harry got a note: "What a pleasant surprise to find my very own *mezuzah*. I no longer have to use the one from my next door neighbor for my daily ritual."

They Came to Teach

Pesakh Fiszman, a Yiddish teacher at YIVO Institute for Jewish Research, and David Fishman, a history professor at the Jewish Theological Seminary, spent four months in Moscow setting up a Jewish studies program at the Russian State University.

"We were bringing back Eastern European Jewish culture to Eastern Europe," Fishman reported to YIVO board chairman Bruce Slovin.

Some of the twenty-five students in Fiszman's class went home and spoke Yiddish to their grandparents for the first time.

At the end of the semester, several students told their American teachers how grateful they were for the opportunity to learn their own language: "Lubavitch came to make us Hasidim. Israelis came to make us go to Israel. You came to teach us for our own sake."

The Real Article

In her heyday, Molly Picon was walking down Broadway when a fan ran up.

"Are you Molly Picon?"

"Yes."

"The original?"

Molly Picon

Is Anybody Listening?

As master of ceremonies of a Reuth dinner, investment banker Ira Leon Rennert felt right at home—he had to plead for attention.

"I don't mind if you talk while I'm speaking. At home nobody listens to me, either."

From Ballet to Comedy

Rita Rudner

Comedian Rita Rudner was a ballerina at age four. "I was terrible," she admits. "In *Swan Lake* I was the lifeguard."

She had to quit ballet when she injured a groin muscle. "It wasn't mine. He's doing very well—he's a soprano with the Vienna Boys Choir."

Rita says she hates Los Angeles. "I don't ever want to go there!"

If *The Tonight Show* calls...

"I'll go!"

Crying in the Temple

Alan Rosenberg, who played the Jewish lawyer Eli on the television series *L.A. Law*, had a brother, Mark, who was vice president in charge of production at Warner Brothers. Mark succumbed to a heart attack at age forty-four while producing a movie called *Fearless*, starring Jeff Bridges.

"I was really torn up about it," Alan said. "My shrink, who was also Jewish, suggested I go to *shul*. Just him saying that made me feel better. I went, I sat, but I couldn't understand the Hebrew. I used to go to Hebrew school, but they never translated for us. It was a matter of how fast we could recite the prayers. So I sat there in the temple and I read the English, and I cried."

Elvis and the Rabbi

Before he died at age forty-two in 1977, Elvis Presley touched a lot of lives, including the rabbi who lived upstairs from the Presley family.

The duplex house on Alabama Street in Memphis was owned by a Mrs. Dubrovner, whose husband had been a *shochet*. The Presleys occupied the ground floor. The father was unemployed and in poor health.

The upstairs flat was rented to Rabbi Alfred Fruchter, the Orthodox leader of Temple Beth El Emeth. The young rabbi and his wife, Jeanette, were good to have as neighbors because they owned two items which the Presleys lacked—a telephone and a phonograph.

On weekends, when Elvis was washing his 1942 Lincoln Zephyr coupe, bought for fifty dollars as a present for his eighteenth birthday, the rabbi would be playing cantorial records, such as Shlomo

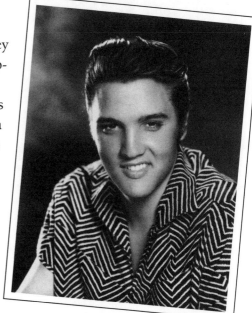

Elvis Presley

Koussevitsky and Moishe Oysher. While taking care of his car, Elvis would listen to the voice of the synagogue wafting from the upstairs window. Has anyone considered the possibility that Elvis might have been influenced by *chazanut**?

It was a hot summer day in 1954 when Elvis knocked on the Fruchter door and asked to borrow the record player. He had made a recording of something called *I Love You, Mama*.

Years later, Fruchter recalled listening to the record being played over and over again in the apartment below. It was an odd sort of song with a strangely rhythmic musical arrangement. The rabbi did not know it, but it was the beginning of the reign of the King of Rock 'n' Roll.

* Liturgy.

Buddy Hackett and friend.

Be Forewarned

If there is one thing Buddy Hackett cannot stand, it is smoking. At a performance at Caesar's in Atlantic City, he reached down to a gentleman sitting ring-side and snatched up a cigar right out of his astonished mouth.

The fearless comedian will not tolerate anyone smoking in his immediate vicinity. But he is fair about it.

"We owe this man a cigar," he announced. "Let's see that we pay him back at the end of the show."

I hope the customer used the money to feed the slot machines rather than his nicotine habit.

Living with Death

At a gathering of Holocaust survivors, Elie Wiesel recalled a story about three people, among them the great author Fyodor Dostoevsky. The three had been sentenced to death for activities against the czar.

The prospect of death affected them in different ways. One of the men lost his mind. The other man's hair turned white. Dostoevsky became epileptic.

Why?

"Because," Wiesel said, "they faced their executioner for one minute. But in this room we have nine hundred men and women who have faced their executioners more than once. They lived not only with death but in death."

Enjoying Jewish Jokes

Dina Merrill says she never wanted to see Jackie Mason's show on Broadway. She does not like "Jewish" comedians particularly. She has never been to the Catskills, where almost all the legendary comedians developed.

Oh, yes, she has seen them in Las Vegas. She even worked with Milton Berle and Alan King. So she knows something about it.

"But it's not my type of humor," she maintains. "I like plays a lot better than standup comedy."

Finally, as she was about to start work with Jackie in *Caddyshack II*, the sequel to the 1980 film, Merrill decided to drop into the Brooks Atkinson Theater to catch Jackie's act.

"I sat there and howled with laughter," she says.

STAN RUMBOUGH

Dina Merrill

So Naive

Gloria Steinem, the feminist leader who wrote a book about being a Playboy bunny, says that a publisher once gave her an advance to write a book about being a hooker on Forty-second Street. She declined the offer and returned the advance.

"I could have kicked myself," she says. "I didn't know that writers don't return advances."

TIM BOXER

Joanna Gleason

Mom's Tough

Joanna Gleason once emceed a fund-raising dinner for Israel Tennis Centers. Her father, Monty Hall, was guest of honor.

"It's a good thing," she told the audience, "you didn't have my mother as the emcee. She would have you renegotiate your pledge and make you hang up your clothes."

No Charge

Isaac Asimov was introduced to a woman who told him she was not married.

"That's a shame," he said.

"Oh, no," said she. "It means I'm free."

"Good," said he. "I'd hate it if you charged."

Company Stands Tall

Carl Glick, who heads a one-man financial firm, testified as an expert for the plaintiff in a court case. At the deposition they asked, "Mr. Glick, what is the name of your company?"

"Carl Glick Company."

"How big is your company?"

"Six feet, four inches."

Lose and You Win

When Lou Weiss helmed the William Morris Agency, he would play tennis with the head of the ABC television network. He would always lose—the sooner to talk business. He convinced the network honcho that it was time to install a woman anchor on the evening news. That is how Barbara Walters became the first woman to anchor a primetime newscast.

"Thank you for losing the tennis game, Lou," Barbara told him.

Barbara Walters

A Certain Call Does It All

Everybody from the Brooklyn-accented Alan King and the English-accented Roger Moore to the German-accented Henry Kissinger and the Southern-accented Dinah Shore joined in the New York Friars tribute to Barbara Sinatra.

It was a lucky thing Jerry Lewis was there.

Actually, when executive director Jean-Pierre Trebot called, the comedian said that he was already committed to a European tour of thirty cities.

"We're talking heavy-duty bucks from a tour like this," Jerry said, declining an invitation to grace the dais.

Then came the call from Frank.

"After we talked," Jerry reported, "I figured who needs all that packing and unpacking?"

Michael Kagen, producer of 9 to 5, with guest star Shannon Tweed.

West Coast Syndrome

Former New Yorkers now ensconced in the Hollywood hills are prone to attacks of nostalgia and longing for the East Coast they abandoned. Take Michael Kagan, who produced the *9 to 5* television series. The Brooklyn native says life is so laid back on the Left Coast that he feels he is on vacation for the rest of his life.

"The only way you know the seasons change is you check the calendar. Granted you don't have to shovel sunshine. But the vitality and energy of New York just don't exist in L.A."

It's All Greek

Robert Wuhl's father died before he had a chance to see his son's success.

He saw his son drop out of college. Robert needed a foreign language to graduate. He took Spanish and failed; he took Portuguese, Latin, even Hebrew. It was all Greek to him.

"I solved the problem by dropping out," he says.

Robert went on to become Robin Williams' fellow deejay Marty Dreiwitz in *Good Morning, Vietnam*. He has since done other films.

"My father did see me on *$20,000 Pyramid*," Robert says. "My parents were at a vacation resort in Florida. He was so excited, he got everybody to watch. That night he died. He saw my entrance into show business. He saw me earn my first paycheck. So he figured he could go to sleep."

How Should He Feel?

At the New York Friars Club, Errol Dante asked George Burns, "How do you feel?"

"From the waist up I'm okay," George said. "From the waist down I need makeup."

George Burns

Becoming a Millionaire

Alan King's son is a clinical psychologist. One day he decided he wanted to become a Donald Trump and make oodles of money. So he joined Merrill Lynch.

"Pop," he said, "I'm going to be a millionaire before I'm forty."

"Only if I drop dead when you're thirty-nine," Alan shot back.

It's Claire, All Right

The Barry Sisters went to Moscow and Leningrad in 1960 on a monthlong cultural exchange. They were part of Ed Sullivan's group, which included opera star Rise Stevens, ballerina Nora Kay, and the Marge and Gower Champion dancers.

TIM BOXER

Claire Barry

"In Gorky Park," Claire recalls, "we did a fantastic show. There were twenty thousand Russians at each performance. Unbeknownst to Myrna and me, there was a vast number of Jews who were familiar with us. They had our records which they taped and passed from one to another underground."

After they returned, the Barry Sisters learned that the Soviets had announced that the popular singing duo perished in an air crash.

"We were devastated," Claire says. "Why would they do that?"

Ever since her sister died of cancer in 1976, Claire has been performing solo, and she meets Russian immigrants all over the United States who can't believe she is still alive.

They come backstage, some with tearful eyes, to get a closeup view of the singer. "We were told you were killed in an airplane crash," one said. "Are you real or an imposter?"

He Also Does Windows

Jack Carter is a fanatic for cleanliness. He loves to wash his car, clean the house, do the laundry and dishes, and vacuum. He is the state-of-the-art house husband.

His compulsiveness drives him to embarrassment. At other homes, he finds himself checking the china, running his fingers on the bar to check for dust, wiping something here and dusting something there.

"I like cleaning house—anybody's," he says. "I clean counters in restaurants. I return trays in cafeterias."

Aware of Jack's compelling habits, Lucille Ball was quite prepared when she invited him for dinner.

Sure enough, Jack lifted his plate to check underneath. He found a note: "You shmuck, it's Wedgewood."

Jack Carter

Introducing Heartburn

Robert Merrill credits Frederick Mann with giving him one of his first jobs. He arranged for Merrill to sing with the Philadelphia Orchestra.

"When Fred was our ambassador to Barbados," Merrill said, "he got tired of beans and rice. He called me to send down chopped liver, lox, and gefilte fish. It was the first time in the history of that country that they got heartburn."

All the Mavens Were Wrong

Jackie Mason

It took Jackie Mason thirty years to become an overnight smash. *The New York Times* finally gave him a decent review of his one-man Broadway show, and Jackie had it made. Until then, he was marked as "too Jewish" for general taste.

For instance, Nat Hiken, creator of such television series as *Car 54, Where Are You?*, caught his act at the Concord Resort Hotel and told him he was the funniest guy around. "If you could lose your accent, you could go on television. Non-Jews will never accept it."

Jackie always was funny, Sammy Cahn said. It took the press thirty years to catch up.

Top to Bottom

Chaim Harari, president of the Weizmann Institute of Science, told a gathering of supporters, "The future of a country is determined by the quality of the people at the top. We must develop opportunities in research for these Jewish scientists coming from the former Soviet Union so they don't go elsewhere."

He illustrated his point with a story about a Jew with a cane. The cane had a golden handle. The man cut off the golden handle.

"Why did you do that?" his friend asked.

"The cane was too long."

"Why didn't you cut the bottom?"

"It wasn't long at the bottom."

You Never Know

Bobby Slayton was sitting in the lobby of the Hotel Pennsylvania in Manhattan when a middle-aged stranger with a briefcase asked, "You're Bobby Slayton, right?

"Yeah."

"You cut me to shreds one night in Napa. I'll never forget it."

Uh oh. The caustic comedian, whose act carries an edge that can rub people the wrong way, assumed a defensive posture.

"You shredded me and my family to bits," the man repeats.

The atmosphere now was getting hairy.

"How do you feel about it?" Slayton asked.

"It was great!" the man said, rushing out to catch a commuter train.

Bobby Slayton

How Do They Miss Him?

After Abe Beame stepped down as mayor of Gotham, he constantly got comments from citizens who missed him.

A man stopped him in a restaurant and said, "Compared to all the scandals going on now, we miss you."

At a funeral chapel, the funeral director said, "We miss you, Mr. Mayor." Abe replied, "How do you mean that?"

Marilyn Michaels

More than a Prince

When Marilyn Michaels was pregnant, Merv Griffin said, "Marilyn, why did you wait until forty to have a baby?"

"Merv," she replied, "when you don't have sex till you're thirty-nine, it's tough."

Marilyn dotes on Mark, now a handsome twelve-year-old.

"My son isn't a Jewish prince," she says. "He's the last emperor."

Her Weakness Revealed

Marilyn Michaels was celebrating her birthday with a cake that her husband, Dr. Peter Wilk, baked himself. Being a surgeon, he is very talented with his hands, even in the kitchen.

When Peter was courting her, he asked what she liked. She said chocolate cake.

Next time he picked her up, he arrived with two mousses he made himself.

"I have a weakness for chocolate," Marilyn confesses. "The way to this woman is through her stomach. It's all right. Peter does surgery for obesity. He makes very fat people thin."

How Will He Manage Now?

Once Elizabeth Taylor was being taken out of Lindy's on a stretcher to an ambulance. Husband Mike Todd was leaning over her solicitously.

"Poor Mike Todd," a waiter remarked. "A woman with a bad back is a woman with a bad back. She's out of commission. I got the same thing at home—she can't cook, she can't clean, nothing."

Elizabeth Taylor

Israeli Ships Don't Sink

When Arnold Forster, general counsel for the Anti-Defamation League, hosted a radio program, *Dateline Israel*, he interviewed a professor from Hebrew University. She was a fervent feminist.

"Listen," he said, "let's say you are on an Israeli ship. It is about to sink. Would you object to the captain saying, 'Women and children first?'"

"Israeli ships don't sink!" she snapped.

Getting Jokes Any Which Way

Jack Carter

Jack Carter went for a medical exam. He stepped on the treadmill. It broke.

"You think you have problems?" the doctor said. "I have Milton Berle in the next room. He's having a cataract removed."

"You mean he's getting a Carter-act removed," Jack shot back.

Over the years, comedians have accused Uncle Miltie of pilfering material.

Henny Youngman came off stage once and cracked, "Berle laughed so hard he dropped his pencil."

We All Belong

Howard Cosell went to Israel in 1985 for the dedication of the Howard and Mary-Edith Cosell Physical Training Center at Hebrew University. He said the most extraordinary thing happened to him while visiting the Western Wall. Someone tapped him on the shoulder and asked, "What are you doing here?"

It was Don Shula, head coach of the Miami Dolphins football team. With him were Bob Griese, Hall of Fame quarterback, and Earl Morrall, also a former Dolphins quarterback.

Howard was flabbergasted. "It was the most incredible meeting I ever had in my life," he told me.

He turned to Shula and said, "The better question is, What the heck are you doing here? At least I'm Jewish!"

This, Too, Is Show Biz

After Eli Wallach was discharged from the army at the end of World War II, he started dating Anne Jackson. One day he asked her if she would help him audition at the American Repertory Theater. He picked a scene where he did all the talking and she only answered yes.

With Anne's assistance, Eli did the audition. The director said, "Thank you very much," and offered Anne a two-year contract.

Finding Immortality

Shelley Winters was married three times. First was Mack Paul Mayer, a Jewish businessman, then two Italian actors—Vittorio Gassman and Anthony Franciosa.

Shelley Winters

Her only child was with Gassman, whose mother was Jewish. Their daughter is Vittoria Gina Gassman, a doctor in geriatrics in Pittsburgh.

The day her daughter gave birth to a son, Ari Joseph, was the day Shelley reevaluated her life. Becoming a grandma for the first time at age seventy does that to you.

"My daughter the doctor," the actress said with pride. "I never had such *nachas*, such joy, till I saw this little boy. I looked in his face and I saw me, I saw my mother, I saw my father.

"You feel safer when you know your grandchildren will know what it means to be a Jew. There is a kind of safety when you understand your covenant with God. That is immortality."

Doubling Your Pleasure

Alan King was emceeing a fund-raising rally at the Waldorf-Astoria during the Six-Day War. The comedian went around the tables, calling upon each person for a donation. He came to an elderly gentleman named Jack Rapoport. Rapoport was a well-known individual on Tin Pan Alley, a popular song plugger and an intimate of Irving Berlin, Jerome Kern, and other songwriters. He was now in his nineties and walked with two canes. He was supported in his old age by friends in the music industry.

Well aware of the man's financial situation, and not wishing to embarrass him, Alan passed him by.

Suddenly a cane shot up in the air.

"Yes, Jack," Alan said.

"Five hundred dollars," Jack announced.

Everyone applauded. That was an enormous amount for this old man.

After all the money had been tabulated, it was decided to raise more. "We never have enough," Alan said.

So they got a shill in the audience to announce "$5,000 plus another $5,000 in memory of my dear departed mother."

One by one, the same people who already donated started to double their pledges in memory of deceased relatives.

Alan was on a roll.

Again he passed over Jack Rapoport so as not to embarrass him. Again the cane shot up in the air.

"Yes, Jack."

Jack stood up and with enormous pride declared, "$500 in memory of the $500 I already gave."

Pearl Harbor Closes a Show

It was 1941 when Red Buttons got his first offer for a Broadway show. He was all set to make his debut on the Great White Way in a show titled *The Admiral Takes A Wife*, a spoof on the American sailors on Pearl Harbor, produced by Jose Ferrer. Unfortunately the show's fate was sealed the day before it opened, not by the barbs of the merciless New York critics but by the bombs of the Japanese.

Red Buttons

Paying for Looks, Not Talent

Film director Larry Peerce says his father would have been happier if Larry turned out to be a doctor or lawyer. His father, of course, was the world-renowned opera tenor and star of the Metropolitan Opera, Jan Peerce.

"My father went through such rejection. It's terrible, so inhumane."

Jan had told his son about auditioning for Earl Carroll's *Vanities* in the early thirties. He stood on a big stage and sang to an empty house. From the audience came the sound of one man clapping.

"Hey kid," the man said, "you're pretty good. We're going to hire you. We'll give you $30 a week."

"That's very low," Jan said.

"If you were six feet tall, we'd pay you $100. And if your nose weren't so big, we'd pay $150."

It's All in the Voice

When Theodore Bikel was in Germany for a performance, he confronted film director Helmut Kauther: "Look, you're my age. Consequently you were there and had to know."

What baffled Theo was the question: How could a people who gave the world Schopenhauer and Goethe follow the barbaric philosophy of Nazism?

Theodore Bikel

Kauther took Theo to a commuter train station in the suburbs. They saw placid housewives, briefcase-toting executives, and business people. It was a benign middle-class scene.

As the train pulled in, Kauther shouted in a sharp stern voice: "Last cars are at the back!"

Everyone ran to the back.

"You see," Kauther said, "it's the tone of voice. Germans follow the tone of voice."

It's Not Fair

Leon Charney, the New York television talk show host, felt quite safe during his two months in Israel during the intifada. He shared the fifteenth floor of the Tel Aviv Hilton with Sylvester Stallone. While Sly was shooting *Rambo III*, Charney was filming a docudrama, *Special Counsel*. It was based on his book of the same name, all about his behind-the-scenes maneuvering at the Camp David peace negotiations between Anwar Sadat, Menahem Begin, and Jimmy Carter.

"Stallone and I would go swimming in the pool," Charney said. "He had a dozen bodyguards. All I had was the defense minister of Israel."

You Don't Have to Be Jewish

Rabbi Marc Gelman of Temple Beth Torah in Nassau County, New York, was working the phones in behalf of United Jewish Appeal. The last person on his list was a Rabbi David Kan on Fire Island.

"I didn't know there was a rabbi on Fire Island, much less a *shul*," he said. He dialed the number.

"David," Gelman said, "I hope you can help UJA this year."

"Last year I gave twenty-five dollars," Kan said. "It was very hard for me. I'm retired. We had an illness."

Gelman was sympathetic and about to terminate the call.

"You know what?" Kan said. "Israel is a cause that is more important than any of us. Israel's needs don't end just because we are having a tough time. I'm going to double my pledge this year."

Gelman was touched. "Don't worry," he told Kan, "I'll pay the pledge."

"No, really, I want to," Kan insisted.

"May God bless you," Gelman said.

"And may Jesus bless you," Kan said.

Gelman dropped the phone.

Kan laughed. "This happens to me all the time. I'm Dutch Lutheran," he explained. "I'm not a rabbi. Nobody can believe a man named David Kan is not Jewish. I even gave to the Lubavitchers. My wife Mary is a member of Hadassah. You have to understand that although all the Jews in the world love Israel, they are not the only people in the world who love Israel."

Dore Schary

Short, But Not Too Short

Arnold Forster, longtime counsel of the Anti-Defamation League, recalls the time Dore Schary appeared at an audience in the early sixties. The toastmaster said, "Ladies and gentlemen, it is my pleasure to introduce the national chairman of the ADL, Dore Schary."

The guest speaker rose, stepped to the podium and, after a long pause, said, "I asked him to make the introduction short—but that was ridiculous!"

Raindrops on His Head

Assaf Harofeh Medical Center, located near Ben-Gurion Airport, had been in need of repairs since it was established as a British military hospital after World War II.

Dr. Jacob Zaidman, director of the clinical laboratory, recounts the story of Israel Galili, a minister without portfolio in the Golda Meir cabinet. He was admitted in the mid-seventies with a leg injury following an automobile accident on the nearby Tel Aviv-Jerusalem highway.

During a rainstorm the roof leaked on his head. When Minister of Health Victor Shemtov came to visit his bedridden colleague, Galili went ballistic.

"You should be ashamed!" he exploded. "Have you ever in your life heard of patients being rained upon?"

In a week, not only was the roof repaired, but the government began construction of a new building.

A Place of His Own

Joseph Gurwin, chairman of the board of UJA-Federation of New York, tells of the time Alexander Abramov came to Yitzhak Ben-Zvi, President of Israel, to present his credentials as Ambasasador of the Soviet Union to Israel.

When Ben-Zvi mentioned that he was born in Russia, Abramov asked, "When did you leave?"

"1901."

"Why did you leave?"

"There wasn't room in Russia for both me and the czar."

"Why did you go? You should have held your ground."

"I had somewhere to go—the czar didn't."

Long and Boring

When Abba Eban made his first public speech in the United States, the chairman of the event apologized for the brevity of his introduction, adding, "I, as your chairman, do not have time to make a long and boring speech because we've invited Abba Eban for that purpose."

After he became Israel's ambassador to the United States and then to the United Nations, Abba Eban's introductions became more effusive. He served a total of nine years. At one of his last dinners as a diplomat, he was introduced: "Abba Eban is well known throughout the civilized world—and also here in the Bronx."

Indeed, the eloquent Abba Eban enjoyed a reputation as a supreme speechmaker in the English-speaking world, which can by generous interpretation be said to include the United States.

Abba Eban

Reading Him Right

Golda Meir

Henry Kissinger visited Israel and Golda Meir greeted him: "We are so proud, Henry, because you are a Jew, a great American, and secretary of state."

"Thank you, Golda. But I must correct you. First of all, I am secretary of state. Second, I am an American. And only third, I am a Jew."

"That's all right, Henry. Here, we read from right to left."

A Jewish Telegram

Itamar Rabinovich, Isaeli ambassador to the United States, could not resist telling a Stalin story at a UJA-Federation dinner in New York.

A triumphant Stalin announced that Trotsky had capitulated. He read a telegram from his Jewish nemesis: "Stalin, you were right. I was wrong."

A Jewish member of the dictator's inner circle corrected him. "No, Stalin, that is not the way to read a Jewish telegram."

"How do you read it?" Stalin asked.

"Stalin, you were right? I was wrong?"

What's in a Name?

Months before the creation of the state, the Irgun needed to send a representative to the United States to obtain arms for the imminent battle with the Arab armies. The British mandatory regime barred all Jews from leaving the country, except for certain political figures and merchants.

Irgun leader Menachem Begin called upon Maks Birnbach, a twenty-seven-year-old businessman in the Tel Aviv diamond market.

Maks Birnbach (center) with Mrs. Zeev Jabotinsky and Menachem Begin in 1948.

Maks, who had came to Palestine from Frankfurt, Germany, at the age of thirteen, was an ardent supporter of Begin's underground organization. He agreed to take on the mission and applied for an exit permit. As a businessman dealing in diamonds, he obtained Exit Permit No. 3. Moshe Sharett, the future foreign minister, held Exit Permit No. 1, and Abba Eban, the future ambassador to the United States and the United Nations, had Exit Permit No. 2.

Peter Bergson, head of the American Committee for a Free Palestine, arranged for Maks to address a gathering at the posh Waldorf-Astoria. He advised Maks to wear a tuxedo. "What's a tuxedo?" Maks said. "In Palestine we don't know from a tuxedo."

At the hotel, Senator Guy Gillette of Iowa, an ardent admirer of Ben Hecht's League for a Free Palestine and staunch supporter of Begin's Irgun, took Maks by the hand and marched him smartly into the Grand Ballroom. The senator cut quite a figure with his six-foot-four frame bedecked in a spiffy black tuxedo. Next to such a distinguished-looking gentleman, Maks seemed like a little boy in an ordinary suit.

A thousand people, all in black tie, stood as the senator strode up to the dais with Maks in tow. They sat down with the likes of Senator Jacob Javits, Congressman Adam Clayton Powell and his singer wife, Hazel Scott, artist Marc Chagall, composer Leonard Bernstein, author Ben Hecht, and Hollywood superstar John Garfield.

Maks was overwhelmed.

In Tel Aviv, he lived across from Mayor Israel Rokach. He used to drive the mayor's little daughter to school on his bicycle. Yet the mayor never once said hello. But here in New York, Maks was mingling with some of the greatest celebrities of the day.

His underground name was Captain Jacoby.

Senator Gillette introduced him as "my close personal friend, Colonel Jacoby."

"I'm not a colonel," Maks whispered.

"Shut up," the senator snapped. "In this country we start with colonel."

The program promised "a special courier from the Irgun."

John Garfield was skeptical. He noticed the cufflinks with the initials MB on "Colonel Jacoby's" shirt. He refused to be hoodwinked.

"I don't believe you're a courier," the actor said in a conspiratorial undertone. "You must be Menachem Begin. You don't have to worry about me, but as a man of the underground, you should be more careful. Your cufflinks will give you away."

At the time, Begin, whose organization was trying to drive the British out of Palestine, was the most wanted man in the Middle East. He had a $50,000 price on his head.

"When Garfield heard me speak," Maks says, "he knew I was no Begin."

Maks, who interspersed his broken English with Hebrew and Yiddish, delivered a succinct message: "Every bullet costs two dollars. How many bullets can I take home tonight?"

Congressman Powell said, "Colonel, if you knew how to speak English you'd have been a disaster."

On that note he started the appeal: "You just heard the language of Jeremiah. How much is that worth to you?"

"Colonel Jacoby" was a huge hit. Mayor William O'Dwyer told him, "If you ever need me, just call."

Four days later Maks called.

The headlines trumpeted the news that police had uncovered fourteen guns in an elevator. They traced the cache to the American League for a Free Palestine.

"Don't worry," the Irish O'Dwyer said. "I'm with Irgun one hundred percent. We both want the British out—from my country and yours."

The mayor made one phone call to his brother Paul, a well-connected attorney, and the guns were released. Those guns went on to help repulse the Arab armies that invaded the newly established State of Israel.

A Good Line

Henny Youngman had only a few lines in *Goodfellas*. Nevertheless, he was so proud that he boasted, "I steal the picture."

"Which frame?" Walter Kirschenbaum asked.

"That's a good line," Henny replied. "I'll steal that, too."

Henny Youngman

Raise Your Hand for Peace

Shimon Peres

There was a time when Seymour Reich, head of the American Zionist Movement, tried to forge unity in Israel. That ill-fated attempt took place during a solidarity rally at the Western Wall.

"I stood between Likud's Yitzhak Shamir and Labor's Shimon Peres. I felt like a referee. So I took their hands and raised them high above their heads like two prizefighters. Suddenly, I felt one of those arms tugging, resisting, like it didn't want to go up."

Years later Reich reminded the prime minister of that incident. "Seymour," Shamir chuckled, "you're so tall. I couldn't raise my arm that high."

What Israel Can Do to You

Radio personality Joan Hamburg tells how a visit to Israel changed her daughter's life. When Elizabeth was traveling with college friends in Turkey, Joan made her a deal she could not refuse: She would pay for the airfare if Elizabeth would meet her in Israel.

"What happened on this trip was extraordinary," Joan says. "By the end of two weeks, my daughter was so changed I was stunned. My child saw a part of herself that was missing.

"We were amazed that in a few months, gone was her non-Jewish boyfriend. This child suddenly became very much a part of the Jewish community and joined a synagogue in Chicago where she lives."

Greeting the Newcomers

The 1990 immigration of Soviet Jews to Israel reminded Eugene Grant of a previous influx of Soviet Jews in 1969. He was in Israel on a United Jewish Appeal mission. In the middle of the night, he was awakened in his hotel room and whisked to Ben-Gurion Airport.

"The first Russians were landing," he said, "and they wanted me to witness the incredible scene. As I watched the immigrants step down the ramp of the El Al plane, tears streamed down my face. It was an emotional experience I never had before."

Grant could not restrain himself. He longed to embrace the newcomers and welcome them to their homeland. He saw a man emerge from the plane and hesitate on top of the stairs. Grant bounded up the ramp. He put his arm around the man's shoulder and tried to reassure him in his best Yiddish.

Eugene Grant

"*Foon vannen kimstu?* [Where do you come from?]"

"*Ich kum foon der cockpit. Ich bin der pilot.* [I come from the cockpit. I am the pilot.]"

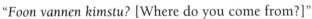

Deep in Thought

Songwriter Sammy Cahn, at his smash one-man concert in San Francisco, stepped aside and gave the spotlight to his trio of backup singers. They performed a medley of Sammy's sweet songs that Frank Sinatra had made famous. Someone asked Sammy what he was thinking about while the trio sang. "The royalties," he replied.

Dressing the Israeli Army

DAVID KARP

Joe Landow

Major Joe Landow had been a staff officer in the Logistics Section of the United States Army in World War II. He was also a lifelong Zionist. So in 1948 he went to Israel and volunteered as logistics adviser to General Yosef Avidan, commander of the Quartermaster Corps. He went to the front lines in the Negev to inspect and advise.

The Yiftah Brigade, a Palmach unit fighting northeast of Gaza, had one company of raw recruits who were Orthodox young men and spoke only Yiddish.

"The men on duty were sitting in trenches less than eighteen inches deep," Landow observed. "There were teams of two, stripped to the waist, one man with his hands on a machine gun looking left and right, and the other man reading out loud. Some were reading the Bible, others the Talmud."

Landow told the commanding officer, "Why didn't you dig that trench deeper? If the Egyptians were alert, these men would be wiped out."

"We have no shovels," the officer answered meekly.

Landow saw to it that they got shovels.

A year later, when the Israel Defense Forces prepared to march in the first anniversary parade on Israel's Independence Day, there was consternation on the highest levels. The soldiers did not have uniforms. What they had was a hodgepodge of civilian clothes and remnants of uniforms from other armies that were brought into the country over the years.

Israel's first prime minister, David Ben-Gurion himself, asked Landow to go back to the United States and obtain summer uniforms for the army of Israel.

"What is the budget for the uniforms?" Landow asked.

"If I had the money," Ben-Gurion shot back, "I wouldn't need you."

Landow's first task in the United States was to organize a network of contributors to raise the necessary cash. He also searched for a factory that could produce the order by the deadline. He found one in the heart of the Bible Belt, a region not known to harbor many Jews. Although the manufacturer was reluctant to accept such a tall order within the time constraints, he invited Landow to dinner to discuss the matter.

When the devout Christian family said Grace before the meal, Landow recited the Shema in Hebrew. He translated, "Hear O Israel, the Lord is our God, the Lord is One," and explained that Jews recite this short prayer morning and night. He also impressed upon them Israel's urgent need for the army of Israel to be properly attired on its special day and that the War of Independence was a stage in the redemption of the Holy Land and the restoration of Zion.

The atmosphere changed from cool civility to warm enthusiasm as the manufacturer readily agreed to fill the order promptly and delay payment. That gave Landow time to raise the funds while the beautifully tailored uniforms made of American cotton from a factory in the South arrived in time for the soldiers of Israel to march in their first Independence Day parade.

Loving Two Women

Alan King, on his way home from Israel, stopped over in London. He appeared on a television show where the host was surprised at Alan's deep devotion to Israel.

"Aren't you an American?"

"Yes, I am."

"How can you have two loyalties? It's like being in love with two women."

"That's right. America is my wife and Israel is my mother."

Isaac Stern

No Time to Waste

When Isaac Stern first played with the Israel Philharmonic Orchestra in 1949, he did concerts every day for the people and the new immigrants. One day he took a moment to visit David Ben-Gurion. He was thrilled to see Israel's legendary leader. But his taxi driver said, "Mr. Stern, don't spend too much time with Ben-Gurion. You have a concert tonight and you have to rehearse."

The Show Goes On

Amiram Rigai was in the middle of a grand performance at Lincoln Center when it happened. A string broke in his piano.

"It was a high C," he said. "I just continued playing as if nothing happened. If it had been a middle C, it would have been a catastrophe."

The same thing happened to Vladimir Horowitz. But the renowned pianist stopped the performance and called for a tuner. It took a half hour to fix it.

"My audience would have walked out," Rigai said. "For Horowitz, they wait."

What Will the Neighbors Think?

Howard Rubenstein, who does public relations for Donald Trump, the *New York Post,* and other prestigious names, started his business as a hostile takeover—just like some of his high powered clients.

"I started in my mother's kitchen in Brooklyn," he said. "And boy, was she hostile!"

He told her when the phone rings to say, "Rubenstein Associates."

"I will not!" she replied. "The neighbors are calling."

Howard Rubenstein

Changing of the Guard

Malcolm Hoenlein has a steady job. He serves as executive vice chairman of the Conference of Presidents of Major American Jewish Organizations. Chairmen of this umbrella group come and go, but the executive vice chairman remains constant.

Malcolm illustrated one change (from Seymour Reich to Shoshana Cardin) with a story about Calvin Coolidge. When the director of the Port Authority of New York and New Jersey died, his deputy called the White House with the news. He woke up Coolidge in the middle of the night.

"I regret to inform you, Mr. President, that the director of the Port Authority has died."

"Is there anything else?"

"Yes. I'd like to take his place."

Coolidge thought for a moment, then said, "It's certainly all right with me if it is all right with the undertaker."

All in the Family

Lou Jacobi was all excited when he came to the Chanukah party of the Minyan of the Stars at the home of playwright Joseph Stein. "Would you believe!" he exclaimed. "Even here, at this affair, we have a scout from MGM. Yes, from MGM—*Mine Gantza Mishpocha* [my whole family]."

The Tourist Trap

How you perceive life in Israel depends on your point of view. Arye Carmon, president of the Israel-Diaspora Institute, says there are two ways of looking at it—from the inside or the outside.

He illustrates with a story about a man who dies and is presented with a choice. He may choose heaven or he may choose hell. Before he makes a decision, he wants to check it out.

Peering through the door to paradise, he sees a lonely Jew sitting under a tree, intently engaged in the Talmud. Boring.

Opening the gate to hell, he is greeted by happy people wining and dining and having a jolly good time. Wonderful! That is for him.

After his arrival, they turn off the lights and throw him into a vat of boiling oil. It was hell!

"What happened?" he yells. "Yesterday this place was terrific!"

"Yeah," they say, "but yesterday you were a tourist."

Testifying to Ownership

Israeli Chief Rabbi Israel Lau is apprehensive about giving up land to appease the Arabs. He feels, as did the state's first prime minister, David Ben-Gurion, that the Holy Land belongs to the Jewish people.

He once asked Ben-Gurion to confirm the testimony he gave to the British Royal Commission of Inquiry headed by Lord Peel. In 1936 Peel went to Palestine to investigate the Arab pogroms against the Jews. He provided a Bible and a Koran for the Jewish and Arab witnesses.

When it came Ben-Gurion's turn to testify, Peel asked, "Where were you born?"

"Poland."

"Very strange. Almost all the Jewish representatives who appeared before the committee were not born in Palestine. Yet you say Palestine belongs to you. Do you have a document to justify your claim?"

Ben-Gurion picked up the Bible and handed it to Peel.

David Ben-Gurion

Knowing When to Speak

Ronnie Dissentshik, director of the Tel Aviv Museum, was slated to speak at an event.

"Speak before dinner," a friend advised. "That way it will be short. Everybody's hungry."

After the speech, Dissentshik turned to his wife Nava and asked how it went. "You could have eaten," she said.

Mayor Shlomo "Cheech" Lahat (right) with former New York City Mayor David Dinkins.

The Power Behind the Man

When Shlomo "Cheech" Lahat was mayor of Tel Aviv, he was driving with his wife, Joyce, one day through the streets of the city. They passed a man digging a trench.

"Didn't you used to date that fellow?" he asked.

"Yes," his wife said.

"See, if you married him you'd be the wife of a ditch digger."

"If I married him he'd be the mayor."

Depends How You Read

Daniel Kaplan, president of the 92nd Street Y, started out working at Barton's, the kosher candy company, while attending Brooklyn Law School at night. Barton's went public in the early sixties, and Kaplan prepared the prospectus. He sent it to the Securities and Exchange Commission (SEC).

"I have a small problem," said the SEC bureaucrat. "I have an aversion to putting the index in the back of the prospectus."

Kaplan was dumbfounded. What difference would it make if the index were in front or back? It would be costly to change it now. He had already printed fifteen thousand copies.

"Who's going to buy our product?" he explained to the official. "Our people. And our people read from the back."

The official promptly okayed the prospectus.

Not Guilty

Sammy Cahn, who wrote the lyrics for such memorable songs as *Three Coins in the Fountain* and *Call Me Irresponsible*, recalled sitting with his father in the synagogue on the High Holidays. They were reciting the *Al Chet*.*

"It always fascinated me," he said, "that these very devout men knew so much about sin that they could list all these sins. How did they know about these kinds of things?"

His father, a man of little humor, turned to his son and said, "I don't know why I'm beating my breast—I haven't done anything!"

Sammy and Tita Cahn

Good Old Days

The world-renowned baritone Robert Merrill watched his son David perform with his rock group, The Rattlers. The girls were screaming in ecstasy.

"He is the sex symbol of the group," the proud papa said. "That never happened to me at the Met."

He was surprised that the rock promoters had provided cold cuts and beer for the performers backstage. "At the Met, I was lucky if they changed the soap every two weeks."

---

* The confession of sins.

Getting Hung Up on Barbra

Record producer Jeffrey Lesser, who has made recordings for the likes of Deborah Harry, Alice Cooper, Sting and Sinead O'Connor, among many other artists, says one of his biggest thrills came early in his career. It was in 1976 when he produced the Barbra Streisand album, *Lazy Afternoon*.

On his first day of rehearsal he went to Streisand's home in Bel Air.

Jeffrey Lesser and singer Dana Mase.

"My heart was pounding," Lesser remembers. "The way the contract read, she could have terminated my involvement at any point during the making of the record. She had the final word. But she was very warm and friendly. Never a tantrum. Never saw her angry. But it was a little nerve wracking just being with her,

"We finally got through the first day of rehearsal. It went well. I walked out the front door, heaved a huge sigh of relief, and through the sheer joy of it all, I flung the car keys in the air.

"The keys got stuck in the tree. I had to go limping back into the house, get a ladder and climb up the tree. It was so embarrassing!"

Never on Yom Kippur

Sammy Davis, Jr., brought up Baptist, converted to Judaism in 1954. While filming *Porgy and Bess* outside Stockton, California, he announced he would not be working on Yom Kippur.

The director turned pale. It would be a $30,000 loss if production were shut down for a day. He rushed to telephone his boss, the fearsome Sam Goldwyn.

The movie mogul then phoned the actor. "What's this I hear, Sammy? You won't be on the set tomorrow?"

"I am a Jew and I don't work on Yom Kippur," Sammy affirmed.

There was a moment of silence.

"God bless you," Goldwyn mumbled, and hung up.

Judges vs. Lawyers

When Stephen Breyer was nominated to the United States Supreme Court, he found the Senate interview quite stressful. He consulted a friend who was a clinical psychologist and stress expert. The friend said he had recently addressed a group of lawyers and judges on that very topic.

He said that as he talked about stress among lawyers, the judges all looked at their watches.

Then he talked about stress among judges, and all the lawyers got up and walked out.

"Where are you going?" he asked.

"Judges don't have stress," the lawyers said. "They *cause* stress."

Shelley's Cousin

TIM BOXER

Shelley Winters

Shelley Winters wanted to cancel her appearance at the thirteenth annual dinner of Friends of Akim.

"I was tired," she told the dinner guests of the organization which supports the developmentally disabled in Israel.

"Then I remembered Gertie. She was a cousin I met when I came to New York from St. Louis when I was nine years old. They told me Gertie was strange because she had been hidden in a barrel when her parents were killed in Austria."

Shelley's two uncles, a rich one named Ben and a poor one named Boruch, brought the child to America. But they did not want to keep her because she was retarded.

"Uncle Ben," Shelley said, "thought Gertie was hopeless and wanted to send her back. But Uncle Boruch got her to the right teachers for remedial education.

"The next time I remember Gertie was when I was in *Oklahoma!* in 1943. She was at the stage door with other kids, waiting to talk to the performers and get autographs.

"Gertie worked in a glove factory. She supported herself and took care of herself. She never asked for a cent."

That is why a weary Shelley Winters dragged herself to this fundraising dinner.

Never on Shabbes

Yiddish actor Ben Bonus once opened a play in Borough Park, a section of Brooklyn heavily populated by Hasidic Jews. They exprerssed their indignation when he scheduled Saturday matinees.

Bonus complained to the chief rabbi: "You closed down the theater! You'd rather have a porno place instead of a Yiddish theater?"

"Yes," the wise man answered. "Our boys would never patronize a porno theater. But you would be a temptation for them on the Sabbath."

Ben Bonus

Reality Check

Albert Hague's wife, Ruth, pitched a movie idea to a youthful studio executive.

"It's about Russians and Americans who detonate an underground nuclear device at the precise same time. The force pulls the earth off its axis and sends it hurtling toward the sun."

The young executive in charge of story development sat up. "Wait a minute. Is this based on a true incident?"

Losing to a Good Cause

Elliot Gould

Shelley Winters recalled the time she toured in a play with Elliot Gould, Ernest Borgnine, and Jack Albertson. Between shows they would play gin rummy.

"I could beat Borgnine and Albertson," she said, "but not Gould."

Once she lost $2,000 to Gould.

"I made him give half to the Actors Studio and half to the United Jewish Appeal."

Pray for the Speaker

Seventy people gathered for a breakfast and lecture at the Jewish Community Center of Fort Lee, New Jersey. The program called for bagels and lox, then a slide show presentation by Tim Boxer on the superstars of Hollywood.

"Do we *bentsch** after the meal or after the speaker?" someone asked.

"You *bentsch* after the meal," Michael Menkin said. "After the speaker you may want to *bentsch goimel***—thank God he's through!"

---

*   Recite the Grace.
** Recite the prayer of Thanksgiving for having escaped calamity.

Speak the Queen's English

Abba Eban says nostalgia is not what it used to be. He spoke in the United Kingdom, where they pronounce schedule as "shedule."

Dwight D. Eisenhower

That reminded him of the time Dwight D. Eisenhower arrived in London in 1940 to take command of the Allied Forces. He kept telling his English secretary to bring his "schedule."

"Of course, General," she said, "it is for you to decide, but I want to tell you that in this country we say 'shedule.'"

That evening he was dining with Winston Churchill at 10 Downing Street.

"General," the prime minister said, "I had the pleasure just now of receiving your colleague, General Omar Bradley. Have you known General Bradley long?"

Mindful of his secretary's warning, Ike replied, "Oh yes, Prime Minister. When we were youngsters, Omar Bradley and I used to go to the same shool."

The Best Speech

Sol Wachtler, former Chief Justice of the State of New York, was the guest at a college luncheon.

"You're not going to give a speech, are you?" a student asked.

"Yes, I am," the judge said.

After the luncheon the judge asked, "That wasn't a bad speech, was it?"

"No," the student said, "but it doesn't compare to no speech."

Full of Gas

Speaking at a dinner of the National Conference of Christians and Jews, Senator Christopher Dodd of Connecticut told about a similar dinner in the past.

William Howard Taft, who served in the White House and later on the Supreme Court, was being introduced by Chauncey DePew, a United States senator and head of the New York Central Railroad. A colorful and loquacious figure, DePew went on and on tediously. Finally he concluded with a description of Taft as "someone who is both pregnant with integrity and pregnant with courage."

Taft finally got up to speak and reassured the audience that "if it's a girl, I shall call her Integrity, and if it's a boy, I shall call him Courage. But if, as I suspect, it is nothing more than gas, I shall call it Chauncey DePew."

What Makes a Minyan?

Robert Harris won first prize at a funniest rabbi contest at Stand-Up New York. He described his sparse congregation in Bronx, where membership totalled a mere fifty-five.

There were times he outnumbered the congregants. He counted women as well as men in the *minyan**—it did not help. He counted empty seats. Sometimes he preached to the janitor.

One day a cat wandered in. He counted the cat in the quorum of ten. "What's the difference? Cat, Katz—sounds Jewish."

---

* A religious quorum of ten.

Behind the Throne

Aya Azrielant is the renowned jewelry designer whose eighteen-karat gold creations are sold in Israel, Japan, and the United States. Her husband and partner, Ofer, is justly proud of his talented wife.

"They say behind every successful man is a woman," Ofer declared at Aya's premiere of a new line of gold designs for an audience of celebrities. "So who is behind the successful woman?"

"A babysitter!" someone exclaimed.

Aya Azrielant

Very Short Lunch

Joseph Stein, who wrote the books for such Broadway blockbusters as *Fiddler on the Roof* and *Zorba*, revealed the birth pangs of *Fiddler*.

Every producer turned it down. He gave one example. He did lunch with a prominent Jewish producer. The man listened patiently as Joe described the plot.

"You mean," the producer said, "this is about a small town, in the middle of Russia, with broken-down Jews, everybody poor?"

"Well, yes," Joe said.

"Does the main character have a love affair?"

"Well, yes—with God. He talks to God a lot."

The producer was dumbfounded.

"I don't have to tell you," Joe related, "it was a very short lunch."

Without Ketchup, You Starve

Shelley Berman

Shelley Berman has fond memories of his grandmother. He learned to cook by watching her perform in the kitchen. His maternal grandma shared a flat with Shelley's parents on Chicago's West Side.

"Even to mash a potato I watched her. She'd throw a little ball of mashed potato in my mouth like I was a bird.

"My mother cooked, but she couldn't hold a candle next to my bubby. My mother had a way of taking a decent piece of meat and drying it out so you couldn't possibly taste anything.

"She gets a piece of meat from the part of the cow that had the least juice. She brought it home, dumped salt on it, drained the whole *neshama** out of it, put it in the oven, and overcooked it.

"She gives it to you and you say, 'Where's the ketchup?' Without ketchup Jews would starve to death. You needed ketchup not just for the taste but for the lubrication. It won't go down your throat. If Vaseline tasted, you'd have that on your steak.

"That was it. That was the way we lived."

Hard to Part

Uri Savir was such a popular consul general, when it came time to leave his New York post to return to Jerusalem many of his friends hosted him at numerous farewell parties. "New York is the only place," he observed, "where at farewell parties you meet new people."

* Soul, spirit.

Pain and Humor

Alan Alda says Jews have a special relationship with suffering. "I never experienced it so much till I sat with Simon Wiesenthal at a dinner."

Alan says that the world-famous Nazi hunter loves jokes. Wiesenthal was in the middle of a funny story when a man came up and said, "You remember me?"

Wiesenthal looked at the man. He remembered him from the camps. They did not say a word. They just nodded. Tears filled their eyes. Then the man walked off.

"Wiesenthal then turned to me and finished the joke," Alan said. "This to me is the Jew's special relationship with humor and suffering. They go together."

ARLENE ALDA

Alan Alda

It Pays to Refuse

Yiddish singer Seymour Rexsite once turned down a fifty-dollar tip— and came away with eight hundred dollars.

It happened at a Catskills hotel where he met Jewish gangster Charlie Gurra (so called because he was fond of barking "Guroutta here"). Gurra gave Seymour fifty dollars to sing *My Yiddishe Mama*. Seymour refused the money but sang the song.

Gurra loved it. He had one of his lieutenants escort Seymour to a craps game in Monticello. Seymour walked away with eight hundred dollars.

Alan Greenberg

A Magical Passover

Alan "Ace" Greenberg is known as the Magician of Wall Street for two reasons. First, he is chairman of Bear Stearns investment bankers. Second, he is an accomplished illusionist. Ace performed his tricks for Minyan of the Stars at a model *Seder* hosted by managing director Michael Silberstein at his Crowne-Plaza Manhattan Hotel.

"A magician at the *Seder*!" exclaimed the irrepressible Irwin Corey. "I never heard of such a thing."

"Passover begins with magic," explained Malcolm Thomson, a former rabbi of Greenwich, Connecticut, now an investment counselor at Sanford C. Bernstein Co. "Moses and Aaron competed with Pharaoh's court magicians in turning staffs into serpents."

Reaching for the Unknown

Hank Greenberg, the first Jew to be elected to the Baseball Hall of Fame, and widely admired for his refusal to play on Yom Kippur for the Detroit Tigers in the 1934 American League pennant race, did not raise his three sons and one daughter in the Jewish faith.

Hank's son, Steve, recalls the day in 1959 when he, eleven years old, and his brother Glenn, thirteen years old, got up to go to school. Their father said they could not go to school that day. It was Yom Kippur. Instead he took them to the Hayden Planetarium.

Hank was reaching out to eternity, but he could not go all the way—to the temple. Religion was not part of him. So he settled halfway, at the planetarium, where he came face to face with the vast universe of the unknown.

Check the Future

Bruce Adler says that when his father Julius came to New York from Tarnigrod, Poland, at age seven, he was under family pressure to go into the millinery trade in the Garment Center.

"My father looked like a combination of Valentino and Joseph Cotton," Bruce says. "At sixteen, he wanted to be an actor. They called him a bum and kicked him out of the house."

For two weeks Julius slept on the fire escape. His mama sneaked food out to him. He got a job in the theater. He brought his first paycheck home. It was bigger than his millinery pay.

Papa looked at the amount and said, "You know, maybe there's a future here."

STAN SADOWSKI

Bruce Adler and Eleanor Reissa in the Broadway musical Those Were the Days.

One Good Turn

The last time I saw Molly Picon perform was in 1980 at the 92nd Street YMHA. A lot of celebrities came to see her show, including Helen Hayes.

"You know," Molly said, "in the Jewish theater I am known as the Jewish Helen Hayes."

"Molly," Hayes replied, "from now I'd be pleased to be known as the shiksa Molly Picon."

Just Thank Mom

Tim Boxer (right) and Uri Savir.

As Consul General Uri Savir presented an award to Richard Dreyfuss on behalf of Beth Hatefutsoth, Tel Aviv's Museum of the Jewish Diaspora, he said this award is more important than the Academy Award.

"The Oscar you get for playing someone else. This award you get for being yourself. For the Oscar, you have a long list of people to thank. For this, you thank only your mother."

Getting the Interview

Alex Haley recalled how he got to interview George Lincoln Rockwell for *Playboy*. It was quite a coup for this African-American writer among whose credits is *Roots*.

First he placed a call to Rockwell. When the neo-Nazi leader called back he said, "I have to ask you one thing. Are you a Jew?"

"No, Methodist," Haley answered.

And that's how he got the interview.

To Write a Book

Irving Wallace, who during his career was the second-biggest-selling author in the world, revealed that he started out writing for magazines and movies. He balked at trying his hand at anything as formidable as a book.

"One day," he said, "while I was collaborating with Jerome Weidman on a script, he told me how to overcome my fear.

"He said to think about writing one page, just one page, every day. At the end of 365 days you have 365 pages—a full-length book in one year."

Since then, Wallace wrote a book a year for thirty-four years.

Irving Wallace

Stop the War

Richard Boone, who starred on television in *Have Gun Will Travel*, recalled a time when he was filming a movie in Israel. It was during the War of Attrition, when planes zoomed overhead toward Jordan and back again.

The noise of the jets in the sky unnerved the crew. Finally an assistant director ran out and shouted into the sky, "Stop the war! We're shooting a movie!"

The Tenth Man

Rabbi Benjamin Blech

Rabbi Benjamin Blech, professor of Talmud at Yeshiva University, told a story about *bashert** that was an inspirational highlight of the Passover lecture series that Rabbi Si Cohen puts together at the Concord Resort Hotel.

He said that one of Rabbi Gifter's students at Telshe Yeshiva in Cleveland was about to be married. The student invited the rabbi and eight other distinguished individuals to the wedding in New York.

Rabbi Gifter and his group boarded a plane in Cleveland. As they approached LaGuardia Airport, the pilot announced that weather conditions were forcing him to divert the landing to Washington.

While waiting in the Washington terminal to resume the flight, the wedding group of nine realized it was time for the *Mincha* afternoon prayer. They asked a security person if he could provide a private room. The guard was stunned by the request, but led the group to a room.

"Are you going to say *Kaddish*?" he asked.

"We need ten to say *Kaddish*," Rabbi Gifter said.

"I'm your tenth. I need to say *Kaddish*."

Afterward, the guard sobbed uncontrollably. He said that he had rebelled against his father and left home a bitter young man. He cut off all contact with his family for years.

A couple of days earlier he was notified that his father had died. Still burning with anger, he refused to go to the funeral. That night his father came to him in a dream and begged him to say *Kaddish* for him.

"I don't believe in it," he told his father in the dream. "Besides, I work at the airport. There's no way I can get to a synagogue."

---

* Preordained, fated, inevitable.

"I beg of you, my son," the father pleaded. "Don't worry, I will send you a *minyan*."

The nine friends finally arrived at the wedding in New York, but they were late. Rabbi Gifter explained to his student, the bridegroom, that he and his fellow passengers were obliged to fulfill a prior engagement in Washington.

What Jewish Mothers Do

Jason Alexander dropped out of Boston University in 1980 in his third year and never looked back. Not only that, but he was also leaving the comfort of his New Jersey home to set up residence in a small studio apartment in Manhattan.

Of course, that broke his mother's heart.

"She wept," Jason recalls. "That's what Jewish mothers do. I was throwing my life away."

He assured her: "Mom, in ten years I'll be doing Tevye on Broadway."

Indeed, in nine years Jason was doing Tevye on Broadway—in *Jerome Robbins' Broadway*.

His parents, Alex and Ruth Greenspan, came up from their home in Coconut Creek, Florida, for the opening. Mom wept throughout the show. That's what Jewish mothers do.

Jason Alexander

Jason continued to find showbiz success as a regular on the smash TV series *Seinfeld*.

An American in Israel

From left to right:
Tony LoBianco, Clyde Dueier,
and Connie Stevens.

Tony LoBianco, an Italian Catholic from Brooklyn whose ex-wife was Jewish, recalls filming in Israel in the midst of the Yom Kippur War.

"I arrived in Tel Aviv two days before the war started. We were going to shoot a film titled *Jacob and Joseph* for ABC-TV, with Colleen Dewhurst and Herschel Bernardi. I played Joseph.

"The director wanted to shut down production and evacuate. I said let's stay, I think we're going to win. I went on television to lend my support. England and France turned their backs on Israel. I'll never forgive them. I was so proud to be an American the day the Americans flew in their aid."

Safeguarding a Marriage

Art Buchwald recalls the time he appeared on the CBS program *60 Minutes*. There was a shot of his wife serving him breakfast in bed.

After the show aired, his wife's feminist friends were fuming. "How could you serve your husband breakfast in bed?" they demanded.

"She was about to cry," Buchwald says, "when she looked around the table at her six liberated friends and realized she was the only one still married."

Selling Bonds

George Jessel once explained how he sold $150 million of Israel Bonds. He never takes no for an answer.

He even sold to a man in Boston, who kept refusing: "I'm not Jewish, my wife's not Jewish, my children aren't Jewish, and my father, *olav hasholem*,* wasn't Jewish."

George Jessel

TIM BOXER

Can She Afford Success?

When folksinger Martha Schlamme made her Town Hall debut, she sent a photo to her father in London. She was dressed in a sexy gown cut out here and there, very fashionable. Her father wrote back, "Hope your success will reach such proportions that you can afford a full dress."

No Prejudice Here

After Sammy Davis, Jr., and May Britt converted to Judaism and married, someone asked the Scandinavian beauty, "Do you believe the people of Sweden will resent your marrying Sammy Davis?"

"The people of Sweden," the actress replied, "are not anti-Semitic."

---

* Literally, "Peace be upon him." May he rest in peace.

The Right Path

Gabe Kaplan, who starred on TV in *Welcome Back, Kotter*, said his father never encouraged him in show business. When Gabe first became a standup comic, he did his act for his father. "What do you think?" Gabe asked.

"Take a civil service test before it's too late," his father said.

"Don't you think I'm funny?" Gabe pressed on. "I want to be a comedian."

"Take the test," his father insisted, "and you'll be the funniest guy in the post office."

Gabe Kaplan

This Is Not for Him

When Theodore Bikel's family fled Nazi Germany in 1938, they settled in Tel Aviv. Young Theo joined Kibbutz Massada, then Kibbutz Gvutzot. Someone had left a guitar behind and Theo taught himself to play. He began singing and playing for his comrades. Soon after he left for Tel Aviv to seek a life in the theater.

"My main job in the kibbutz," he says, "was standing around on heaps of manure. I really had very little aptitude for agriculture."

Opening His Eyes

Howard Cosell, who grew up in Brooklyn, did not have a Jewish education. His Jewish consciousness was not raised until he witnessed the slaughter of eleven Israeli athletes by Palestine Liberation Organization terrorists at the 1972 Olympics in Munich.

"That's how I got so deeply involved in Israel," he said. "I left those games knowing who I was. I knew that forever more, no matter what happened in my life, I was Jewish—and very proud of it."

Howard Cosell

CAPITAL CITIES/ABC, INC.

This One's a Brain Surgeon

As Isaac Stern was getting an honorary Ph.D. from Ben-Gurion University, Zubin Mehta turned to the violinist's wife, Vera, and cracked, in Yiddish yet, "That's all the Jews need—another doctor!"

He Was Always There

Jackie Mason singles out Red Buttons for standing behind him in his darkest days. When Jackie's career was on the skids, Red would always come over and encourage him to stick with it. He would tell Jackie he was brilliant and funny, and some day he'd make it.

"Now that I'm a sensation," Jackie says, "I don't hear from him!"

A Fishy Tale

Our British cousins are different from us in more ways than one. Take "The Case of the Gefilte Fish."

Judge Aron Owen is a Welsh Jew who sits on the highest court in London. When he was a barrister, he represented a man who was involved in a divorce case. Aside from the couple and the barrister, no one else was Jewish.

Cruelty was alleged by both sides. For instance, the man claimed his wife served him fish and he did not like it.

"Oh, you don't like fish, do you?" the judge inquired.

"No, my lord, I do."

"Ohhh, was something wrong with the fish that she gave you?"

"Yes."

"What was wrong with it?"

"Well, my lord, she put sugar in it."

The other barrister and solicitors were mystified. Not Owen. He realized that the husband was either a Pole or a Litvak who does not like sweet gefilte fish. Owen dropped his head on his papers to stifle a laugh.

"What did you say?" the judge asked.

"My lord, she put sugar in my fish."

The judge picked up a red pencil and wrote, "Sugar in the fish," and underlined it—"cruelty."

Raising Money Effortlessly

When Technion presented an honorary doctorate to Larry Tisch, the occasion reminded St. John's University head Father Flynn of the time one of his priests had to raise money. The priest needed $30,000 to buy a rare Hebrew manuscript for the school's Catholic library.

He called Samuel Belkin, then president of Yeshiva University. Father Flynn explained that Belkin was renowned for his effortless way of separating Jews from their money.

"No problem," Belkin said. "Give me a week."

Less than a week later, the rabbi called the priest: "I got you $30,000. Congratulations."

"Gee, rabbi, that's wonderful. Tell me, how did you get it so fast?"

"That was easy. I called Cardinal Spellman."

Laurence A. Tisch

What's Better than Man?

Dominick Pupura, dean of Albert Einstein College of Medicine at Yeshiva University, says that as a scientist, he has no problem with Creation.

"I believe God created man and then, in a state of euphoria at that achievement, overdid himself and proceeded to create something better—woman."

Rebirth of a Soul

Ron Leibman, who was raised in New York with no Jewish education, says his Jewish consciousness was finally aroused when he made a two-week trip to Israel to shoot a promotional film for United Jewish Appeal.

At Yad Vashem, one scene blew his mind. He gazed at a collection of photographs taken by a German soldier in the Warsaw Ghetto on a "normal" day. Ron looked at everyday scenes—cars and buses, people bustling, and in the midst of all this life, children dying in the street.

There was one particular picture that moved Ron to tears. It was a little girl, in rags, sitting on the curb, totally abandoned.

Ron went to the Chaim Weizmann Memorial. He watched a group of school girls, in blue and white uniforms, arrive at the memorial.

"One little girl sat down on the side to rest. It was the same face as that little girl in the Warsaw Ghetto. I understood all in that moment. This was the rebirth of that child who was forced to die because of those Nazi bastards. And now there is an Israel where this child can live. It was a very powerful experience that I shall never forget."

Ron Leibman

Shirk Responsibility and End Up a Genius

Leo Rosten is continually amazed how culturally prolific the Jewish people are. A small minority, yet they produced novels, philosophical writings to match anything the world has known. Why? How?

He attributes such high achievement to the fact that learning is so venerated among Jews.

He illustrates from his own childhood in Chicago. Whenever there was a chore to be done, such as taking the ashes out of the furnace and carrying them out to the back alley, he would bury his head in a book.

His father would pat him on the head and say, "Lay in stock. Build inventory. Soak up wisdom. That's more important than ashes in the furnace."

ARTHUR RUBENSTEIN

Leo Rosten

Burglar on Vacation

There was a man in Israel known as Moishe the Burglar. Any town he went to, if there was a break-in, the cops would haul him in. Ninety-nine percent of the time they were right—he turned out to be the perpetrator.

Once he went to Eilat for a rest. There was a rash of burglaries. Naturally the cops brought him in for questioning. That upset him very much. He insisted he was innocent.

"I'm a burglar," he admitted. "But here I'm on vacation."

Always a Crisis

When Leon Uris was writing *Exodus*, he would get frequent calls from his editor. Every time a crisis flared in the Middle East, the editor would call frantically for the manuscript. He wanted to bring the book out while it was hot.

"Don't worry," Uris assured him, "whenever I finish the book there will be a crisis."

Leon Uris

Garbo's Death Wish

Greta Garbo wanted to be laid to rest next to film director Maurice Stiller, who was buried in a Jewish cemetery in Stockholm. He was the Jewish man who discovered Greta Lovisa Gustafsson and first presented her on the screen as Greta Garbo.

Stiller was born Mowscho Katzman in 1883 in Helsinki, Finland, and became active in Sweden's budding film industry. He discovered Garbo as an eighteen-year-old actress in one of his movies. They became inseparable and traveled together. Two years later, in Berlin, they met Louis B. Mayer, who hired them both to work at MGM. The rest is history.

Stiller returned to Stockholm, where he died in 1928.

When Garbo made known her wish to be buried, Rabbi Mordecai Lanxner sent her a letter explaining that Jewish law did not permit her, as a Christian, to be buried in a Jewish cemetery—unless she converted.

He did not hear from her again.

Humor the Best Defense

During the Persian Gulf War of 1991, when missiles rained on Tel Aviv, Topol was starring in *Fiddler on the Roof* on Broadway. He telephoned his son Omer, a film director in Tel Aviv.

Omer told his father not to worry: "The safest place is Jerusalem—Saddam Hussein would not dare bomb the Holy City. Then again, seeing how inaccurate his missiles are, maybe the safest place after all is Tel Aviv."

Topol

Talking to the Wall

Lawrence J. Epstein, an English professor at Suffolk Community College in Selden, New York, had an interesting student in Mendy Berger. Mendy was a Long Island jeweler and Holocaust survivor. He remembered vividly how he shoveled corpses in a death camp.

"Do you still believe in God?" Epstein asked.

Berger answered by relating how, after the war, he married a woman who had been tortured with terrible medical experiments in the camps. For twenty years they tried in vain to have children.

They visited Israel in 1967. His wife was tired from sightseeing, so Berger walked to the Wall alone. He stood there crying, wondering why he was so unfortunate. A bearded young man told him to stick a note into the Wall.

Berger wrote "I want a child" on a piece of paper and stuck it in the Wall. He turned to the young man, but he was gone.

Ten months later his wife gave birth to a daughter.

Howard Squadron (right) and Seth.

Keeping an Audience

When Howard Squadron came to the Pierre Hotel to act as chairman of an American Jewish Congress dinner, a friend asked, "What are you going to speak about?"

"I'm not making any speeches," the lawyer said.

"Good," his friend said. "We'll stay."

Yiddish in Warsaw

"It's a shame!" exclaims Zypora Spaisman, a star of the Folksbiene Theater. "American Jews don't patronize the Yiddish theater. But when they visit Warsaw, they feel compelled to go to the Yiddish theater there. And almost all the actors aren't even Jewish."

When the Warsaw Yiddish State Theater came to New York, Zypora did not exactly welcome them. She told the actresses, "Your grandfathers killed Jews, and now their granddaughters are playing how to be Jews."

Well Known at the Concord

Alan Dershowitz was once crowned "the lawyer of last resort" by *Time* magazine. When an Israeli paper printed that designation, it came out in Hebrew as "the last resort lawyer in America."

Alan Dershowitz

Why Look for Problems?

At the Sharon Group of Hadassah luncheon at The Plaza, I sat with Julie Berke. She is a representative of the French designer Louis Feraud. Her husband, Herman, now retired, owned shipping tankers.

Julie said she's the first non-Jewish member of the Hadassah group.

She hasn't converted yet?

"I tried twenty-three years ago."

At that time she went to Manhattan's Central Synagogue and told the rabbi, "I just married a Jew and I want to convert."

"Are you happy?" the rabbi asked.

"Yes, very happy."

"So why change?"

Going Straight

Rabbi Yitzhok Grossman is a famous personality in Israel, where he runs Migdal Ohr, a school that rehabilitates dropouts, the dispossessed, and other members of the underclass. He earned a reputation as the Disco Rabbi because he looked for troubled youngsters in nightclubs and bars to rescue them from a life of crime and despair.

Nachman Farkas was for many years infamously known as Israel's Willie Sutton. He was a petty thief who escaped from one prison after another. His prison breakouts were breathlessly chronicled in the newspapers and captured the imagination of the entire country.

For two decades his misfortunes kept this pathetic comic-strip-like character behind bars for various periods of time. Then he dropped out of the public eye. He lived a hermit's life in the forests. He tried raising goats. He was unhappy.

Finally he came to Migdal Ohr and poured his heart out to Rabbi Grossman. "They made a hero out of me," he said, "but that's far from the truth. I am now divorced. My son is in an institution for delinquents. I am an alcoholic. The police are looking for me on a two-year-old charge of disorderly conduct."

Farkas looked much older than his fifty-six years. The strain of his criminal career was etched on his face. He was a broken man.

"All I want is a quiet life," he pleaded. "I want to show criminals and youth what can happen if you don't go straight."

The Disco Rabbi listened to the reformed thief. Then he got up and said, "We will help you."

This Check's Not Enough

Ed Koch presented to Dr. Ruth Westheimer the Bezalel Academy of Art's Jerusalem Prize in the form of a $10,000 check.

"I'm going to divide this money to three charities I work with," Dr. Ruth said.

"You're going to give part to Bezalel?" Koch asked.

"No," she replied. "I am not going to take and give back. On the contrary, I am going to come back and ask for more."

Dr. Ruth Westheimer

Now That's Loyalty

Herman Zvi Hirsch was a butcher by trade, a very modest man, and a devoted Jew who attended a *shtiebel** on the East Side every day until he died at ninety-one.

Jerome Hornblass, a justice of the New York State Supreme Court who worships at the same *shul*, delivered the eulogy. He was startled to see Donald Trump in the sparse audience. It was a rainy morning, yet this real estate megamogul had driven from his Fifth Avenue domain all the way to Sinai Chapel in Flushing, Queens, to join in the mourning of a little-known Orthodox Jew.

"What brings you here?" the judge asked. "Did you know Zvi Hirsch?"

"His son Bill works with me," the real estate developer replied, "and he's a great guy."

* An intimate, cozy synagogue, usually a prayer room in a rabbi's house.

Doesn't Everyone Have a Nurse?

Phil Silvers had three daughters at a late age. One night his youngest woke up screaming from a nightmare.

"I got lost, Daddy!" she wailed.

Silvers comforted the little girl: "I know, honey. I got lost too when I was a little boy. I was walking to school and I turned down a street, and then I turned down another street, and then I turned down another street, and I went to the corner and—I was lost."

"Where was your nurse?" the kid asked.

Phil Silvers

Have Chair, Will Play

Amiram Rigai, the great Israeli concert pianist, now living in New York, gives concerts in Israel every year. But he is not enamored with the piano stools they provide in Herzliya and the other places. They are either too high or too low.

"I don't mind their pianos." he says. "I don't expect grand pianos like we have in the United States. But definitely I would like to sit on a good chair.

"You have to sit for an hour and a half in concert. If you are not comfortable, how can you perform? Wherever I went, I carried my own piano stool from home."

CHRISTIAN STEINER

Amiram Rigai

Forty Years Equals Four Hours

Lisa Belzberg, chair of Israel Bonds New York New Leadership, acknowledged the influx of Russian Jews to Israel: "Some will debate what's worse—forty years in the desert or four hours on Aeroflot."

Thinking Ahead

Red Buttons' father died at ninety-three. Two years before, Red asked, "Pa, what does a man of ninety-one think about?" His father said, "Ninety-two."

Poems Open the Heart

DAVID KARP

Yehuda Amichai

There was a fellow who borrowed a book of Yehuda Amichai love poems. He had a date and thought it would help.

Later he was asked about the date. "It worked," the fellow said. "I'm engaged."

Amichai does not protest when he is used that way. "When I hear someone just used me, I'm happy," he says. "That is what my books do. Besides, I really believe poetry should be used—better than being neglected."

What the Seder Teaches

Marc Weiner tells about the time he became a *baal teshuva*.* He went to his first *Seder* at the home of a friend.

"I thought, great, what a meal! Then I notice what's on the plate—a burned egg, a bare bone. Boy, the recession sure hit hard in this house."

Marc was ambivalent about the *afikomen*** custom: "It teaches children three things: thievery, bribery, extortion."

He noted that the *Haggada* speaks of four sons: the wicked, the stupid, the spaced out. "This is not a family—it's the Three Stooges!

"Finally you have the wise kid, a doctor—obviously adopted."

---

* A returnee to the practice of Judaism.
** From the Greek, meaning "dessert." A piece of matza put away to be eaten at the end of the *Seder* meal. Traditionally, children hide the matza and return it only on the promise of a reward.

Just in Jest

Writers and Artists for Peace in the Middle East came to praise Ron Silver, but some of his colleagues came to bury him—in jest. Tony Randall dug right in with a shovelful of mirth.

"I've known Ron since he came out of college," Tony said. "He studied in Taiwan, where he earned a degree in Chinese. He speaks eight languages. There is hardly a subject he has not studied—except acting."

Ron Silver

His Choice Seat

One of hotel operator Sam Domb's pet projects was the building of Young Israel of Jamaica Estates, a synagogue in Queens. Instead of reserving for himself a permanent seat in front of the Ark, Sam sits in the very last row. "I don't want anybody talking behind my back," he says.

Oh, Happy Day

Michael Sonnenfeldt, chairman of the board of American Associates of Ben-Gurion University, says, "The happiest day of my life was the day I bought my boat—and the day I sold it."

Sleeping in Brooklyn

Gary David Goldberg

Gary David Goldberg, the successful Hollywood producer of such television series as *Lou Grant* and *Family Ties*, has fond memories of his youth in Brooklyn.

He remembers the small apartment and the bedroom he shared with his brother Stanley. Gary slept near the door, Stanley near the window.

"Why do I have to sleep near the door?" Gary asked.

"This way," his brother said, "if someone comes to rob us, they get you first."

Watch Your Language

When Senator Daniel Moynihan paid a visit to the Bobover Rebbe in Borough Park, Brooklyn, the rebbe said, "I'm sorry my English isn't too good."

"Your English," the senator said, "is far better than my Yiddish. The only Yiddish I know is what I picked up on the street as a boy—which I wouldn't repeat in front of a rabbi."

"I picked up some English that way, too," the rebbe said. "But I wouldn't use those words in front of a senator."

A Lifetime Responsibility

Eric is the youngest of Kirk Douglas's four boys. "That means," Eric says, "even when I'm sixty years old I'll still have to say *Ma Nishtanah*."*

Speaking Doesn't Mean Knowing

Art D'Lugoff learned Hebrew at Yeshiva of Flatbush in Brooklyn.

In conversation with a couple of Israelis at the Village Gate, his Greenwich Village night spot, Art sprinkled his talk with Hebrew words.

The Israelis were surprised. "You understand Hebrew?"

"No," Art said. "I only speak it."

Jackie's Woman of Valor

Jackie Mason had a bachelor party before he married his manager, Jyll Rosenfeld. "I came here," community activist Rev. Al Sharpton said, "to make sure that it was not an interracial marriage—black people have been abused enough!"

Attorney Shannon Taylor reminded Jackie to recite *Ayshet Chayil* every Friday night. The Sabbath poem speaks of a woman of valor being worth more than rubies, sapphires, emeralds—"all the things you'll have to buy her."

---

* "Why is this night different?" Recited by youngest member at the Passover *Seder*.

His Last Visit to Mother

Paul Sorvino

Paul Sorvino came to a luncheon of the Israel Cancer Research Fund at The Plaza. At that very moment, his mother, Marietta, her body ravaged by the dreaded disease, was fighting for her life in an East Side hospital.

"I'm losing her," Paul whispered, his eyes clouded with sadness.

"I came to celebrate my mother's life, even though she's close to death, and to celebrate the hope that soon there will be a cure for this terrible disease."

The actor, of Italian heritage, recounted his Jewish connection growing up in the Italian-Jewish neighborhood of Bensonhurst, Brooklyn, where he was the local Shabbes goy. He had so many Jewish friends that he was able to write a term paper on Zionism.

"I've even been to Israel—I've paid my Jewish dues."

Paul had been going to the hospital every day to be with his eighty-four-year-old mother. "We almost lost her a couple of days ago," he said.

He looked at his watch. It was 2:30 P.M.

He bolted out the door and ran to the hospital for his daily vigil. It would be his last visit. His mother had died—at 2:30 P.M.

Better than Leeches

The first time Bob Saget went to Israel, he took his wife Sherri. The second time, he took his parents along with his wife. He was especially delighted to be able to share the experience with his mother and father.

Bob's most emotional moments were with his father, Ben, at the Western Wall.

"We went several times. Whenever the women said they're going to the bathroom, my father and I said we're going to the Wall.

"You're outside, praying at a temple outdoors. You feel people releasing their pain. What you can't do in a shrink's office, you can do at the Wall. It's a spiritual outlet. Better than leeches!"

Bob Saget

There Are More Ribs

Robby Berman is a member of a unique club—he's an Orthodox comedian. There aren't many of them around. Born in Brooklyn and raised in Woodmere, Long Island, he now lives in Israel. He did his stint in the army. His rank? "AWOL," he says.

Actually he was injured during training. He had surgery in Dallas, where they removed two ribs.

"Now I'm studying Kabbalah," he says, "trying to figure out how to make two women out of them."

Everybody's a Star

Larry Kert

Larry Kert first tasted show business at age five when he was cast as Fredric March's son in the 1935 film *Les Misérables*.

"I was an extra," he said. "I brought in extra money for the family. My father was a bookkeeper. My mother registered all the kids with Central Casting so everybody could bring in the extra $8.50 a day."

Holy Autographs

When Mickey Rivers was a star center fielder for the New York Yankees, he did an unusual *mitzvah* for a group of youngsters.

Norman Liss was commissioner of the Riverdale Jewish Center baseball league, and arranged for Rivers to appear at their breakfast. Unfortunately, Rivers forgot to bring photos. Some three hundred kids were about to be disappointed, for in the past every ballplayer brought pictures to autograph.

"The only thing in the synagogue that was available was Hebrew *benchers*,"* Liss recalled. "Rivers signed the *benchers*, which contain prayers for meals. There are now three hundred kids, including my own son Michael, who have the most unique documents in existence—Mickey Rivers *benchers*."

---

* Book containing Grace After Meal.

Prejudice from Within

"Do German Jews still forbid their children from marrying Polish-Russian Jews?" Milton Berle wondered aloud as he related the downfall of his father due to such prejudice.

His parents were native New Yorkers. His father, Moses Berlinger ("man of Berlin"), met Sarah Glantz at a dance in 1899 and fell in love. Sarah's parents came from Russian Poland.

Moses' family were status-driven members of the well-heeled, long-established German-Jewish community, and vigorously opposed this union. Moses was a member of the board of directors of Ex-Lax, one of the biggest companies in the country. His relatives on the board warned that if he went through with this marriage they would destroy him.

"Father defied them," Milton said. "His family disowned him, broke him, and threw him off the board. He wound up a twelve-dollar-a-week salesman, selling paint for Sherwin-Williams. It was a sad affair. Due to the abuse he got from his family, my father was not well for thirty years. He died from a heart attack."

Milton Berle

The World According to Ron Silver

At an Israel Bonds Sabra Society dinner, Ron Silver summed up his view of the world: "There are two types of people in the world. There are Jews and the others who worship one."

Intelligence Saves the Day

Uri Lubrani, once Israel's ambassador to Ethiopia, not only master-minded Operation Solomon but also saved the mission from premature termination.

In the midst of the twenty-four-hour rescue of 14,500 black Jews in May 1991—six planes bound for Israel already had taken off from Addis Ababa—a hitch arose.

"The prime minister wants to know where the money is," an Ethiopian official demanded.

Uri, on behalf of the Israeli government, had promised the Ethiopians thirty-five million dollars to redeem the Jewish population.

"Did you give me a bank account number?" Uri asked.

"No," the official said. "I forgot."

The official called his superiors. But both the prime minister and finance minister were new, and neither knew the account number. And the former dictator had just fled the country.

"Do not worry," Uri assured the finance minister. "You will have your money as soon as you give me a bank account number. Can you imagine that an entire nation wants to cheat you out of a miserable thirty-five million dollars?"

The official was flustered, but finally came up with a brilliant idea: "You [Israel] have excellent intelligence. You tell me what our account number is in New York."

Uri called Jerusalem. Within the hour he had the government's account number and more—the name of the bank officer in charge of the account. The money was deposited and an hour later the rescue operation was concluded.

A Rosa by Any Other Name

Tovah Feldshuh, who gets mail addressed to Tovah Vulture and Torah Feldshuh, was invited to entertain at a Reuth dinner.

"What would you like me to sing?" she asked president Rosa Strygler.

"Look, Tuna, you can sing anything you want," Rosa said.

Tovah Feldshuh and son, Brandon, and daughter, Amanda.

What's the Rush?

Broadway producer Arthur Cantor had a mother who continually nagged him to get married. Finally he brought home a woman. His father was delighted with the prospective bride. Mother, however, was aloof.

"What's the matter, ma?" Arthur demanded. "She's nice, she's Jewish, and she doesn't smoke. You always wanted me to get married. What's wrong?"

"What's the hurry?" Mom replied.

World's Best Psychiatrist

Fyvush Finkel

Fyvush Finkel says he has two pleasures: "I buy the most expensive cigars and I go to the synagogue. I'm there morning and night."

When he's not in Hollywood filming the *Picket Fences* television series, you can catch him at the Sutton Place Synagogue in his East Side neighborhood.

"My colleagues in show business," Fyvush says, "spend fortunes going to psychiatrists. My 'psychiatrist' doesn't charge me a penny. And I get better results. I have no hangups."

Not Fair

Freddie Roman compared Christmas to Chanukah and found that the Jews come out short—and never mind that we get eight days of presents while gentiles get only one day.

Every year Christmas comes precisely on the twenty-fifth day of December. Every year it is the same. You can make plans.

Jewish holidays never come on time. What Jew hasn't said, "Chanukah is early this year?"

Rosh Hashanah was early, too. It did not come the same time as last year. Unless you have a Manischewitz seven-year calendar, you never know when it will come.

The Shirt off His Back

Rafi Hochman, the mayor of Eilat, is joining in his city's exemplary effort to integrate Russian *olim** into the community. His wife has given away half of his shirts.

"If I see in the street a familiar shirt," Rafi says, "I know it is a new immigrant."

Excellent Choice

Myrna and Harvey Frommer, authors of *It Happened in the Catskills*, were at the Concord one afternoon when they overheard a couple checking in.

"What room would you like?" the clerk asked.

"The dining room," they answered.

So Give Again

Morris Weissbrod recalls a favorite story of John F. Kennedy. The President advised everyone in the White House to exercise, so Secretary of Labor Arthur Goldberg went mountain climbing. When his group came down the mountain, Goldberg was missing. A search party was sent up.

"Secretary Goldberg," they shouted, "this is the Red Cross."

A voice came booming down: "I already gave at the office."

---

* Literally, "those that are going up" (to Jerusalem). Immigrants to Israel.

Gabriel Erem and Rabbi Menachem Schneerson.

Nothing's Forgotten

Gabriel Erem, publisher of the elegant *Lifestyles* magazine, says he got a call from Rabbi Shmuel Butman, head of the Lubavitch Youth Organization, inviting him to a *pidyon haben** for his first grandson.

At the time of the *simcha*,** Erem was at a Holocaust memorial meeting at Park East Synagogue with Abe Foxman, national director of the Anti-Defamation League, and Shoshana Cardin, chairman of the Conference of Presidents of Major American Jewish Organizations.

They all trekked to Brooklyn for the celebration. Before heading back to Manhattan, Rabbi Butman persuaded the trio to drop in on Rabbi Menachem Schneerson, the Lubavitcher rebbe.

Cardin was reluctant to go. "I was here four years ago, I stayed on line, I saw the rebbe for four seconds, I asked him a question, he said he'll mail me his response. You know what? I'm still waiting."

"You're the leader of the Jewish community in America," Erem said. "You must go."

They walked four blocks to 770 Eastern Parkway. Cardin was in short sleeves so Erem borrowed a shawl from a lady on line.

In the hallway the rebbe was leaning on a table, listening to each person presented to him and handing out charity dollars. As Cardin approached, the rebbe looked her in the eye and said, "Mrs. Shoshana Cardin, you came to me four years ago, you asked me a question, and I still owe you a letter."

* Literally, "redemption of the son," a biblical ceremony of redemption of the mother's first-born son so he will not be required to devote his life to Temple service. Ritual involves payment of silver coins to a *Kohen* (priest).

** A festive celebration, a party.

Same Old Story

David Brenner grew up amidst anti-Semitism in Philadelphia. He had fist fights every day on his way to school.

"Why do you hate me?" he asked one kid.

"You killed Christ."

"That was two thousand years ago."

"I just heard it today."

David Brenner

Sings Great—If You're Deaf

Frank Buchweitz, former executive director of Hebrew Institute of Riverdale, enjoys leading Shabbat services.

"I'm the world's greatest *chazan**—for the hard of hearing," he quips. That tells you what kind of cantor he is—or what kind of *kibbitzer.***

"Sometimes I sing flat, sometimes I'm off key. The older people think I'm terrific. They say I'm wonderful. Of course, the older they get the less they hear."

Frank lost out on conducting the Passover *seder* at a resort. They opted for a professional cantor.

Frankly, he couldn't understand it. "Why should they pay him so much when they can hire me for nothing? Furthermore, I pray better. A *chazan* stretches it out. I get to the main part of the *Seder*—the meal—faster!"

---

* Cantor.
** Joker.

Lionel Hampton (left) and Sammy Cahn.

Did David Boogie-Woogie?

Lionel Hampton did concerts in Israel with his twenty-five-piece orchestra and donated the money to Magen Dovid Adom.

He asked Chief Rabbi Isaac Herzog, "Rabbi, do you know what I play?"

"You play bebop jazz and boogie-woogie," Herzog replied. "David played before you."

Herzog gave him a prayer to say before the shows. It was the *Shehecheyanu** blessing.

"I had the piece of paper with the prayer on my vibes," Hampton said, "and the wind just took that paper away. I did it anyway. They said they never heard the prayer uttered that way before."

Don't Stop Now

Isaac Stern was introduced with so much enthusiasm at a UJA-Federation fund-raiser in New York that he protested: "No one is really as good as he is made out to be in his introduction."

He recalled when Abba Eban was being introduced so effusively he was humbled by the enormous outpouring of praise. Stern asked Eban how he felt about the adulation.

"Listen, Isaac," he answered, "at occasions like this, you look down like you're slightly embarrassed. But what you're really thinking is, 'Is that all they can say about me?'"

---

* Literally, "Who has kept us in life." A prayer of gratitude and celebration, recited on the eve of a holiday and other special occasions.

Breaking into Show Biz

Sid Caesar started his comedy and acting career as a musician. Not that he planned it that way. You see, his father, who owned a diner in Yonkers, came home one day and said, "Sidney, you are going to learn to play the saxophone."

"How come, dad?"

"Because somebody left one in the store."

Sid Caesar

Spitting on Target

Red Buttons started out singing in the choir of the famed Cantor Yossie Rosenblatt. The choir performed in Borough Park, Brooklyn, and the Old Romanian Shul on Rivington Street on the Lower East Side, which is now a tourist attraction.

Red was recently in the neighborhood. He was showing a friend the *shul*, one of the oldest in New York. At that moment, out came a group of Hadassah women with a guide carrying a megaphone.

"Ladies, ladies," the guide shouted. "Look who's coming—the great actor, the great comedian, who sang in this synagogue with Rosenblatt in the twenties."

"How did you know that?" Red asked.

"I was in the choir with you."

They both remembered the choirmaster, Cooperman, who used to spit.

"When Cooperman didn't like what you were doing," Red said, "he'd bang on the table and spit across the room. I think they got the Norden bomb sight from him."

Martin Charnin

Martin Charnin has made a successful life on Broadway. Among his achievements are being the lyricist and director of *Annie*. His father, on the other hand, loathed the American musical theater with a passion.

His father was a *basso profundo* at the Metropolitan Opera who sang with Ezio Pinza. When Pinza quit the Met to star in *South Pacific* on Broadway, the elder Charnin never talked to him again.

Pinza would come to the Charnin home and bang on the door. Martin's father would come to the door and say, "Charnin isn't home!"

When Martin got a role in *West Side Story* in 1957, he could not tell his father. He had just finished college as an art major. He would get up early every morning and say he was going downtown to look for a job as art director in advertising. Of course, he was going to rehearsals.

Finally came the day when the show was going on its out-of-town tryout. Martin had to tell the truth. He sat his father down and broke the news gently.

"Look, pop," he said. "I'm in a Broadway musical. But listen. Anybody who has anything to do with it is Jewish. Jerry Rabinowitz (Jerome Robbins) is the choreographer, Arthur Levine (Laurents) wrote the book, Stephen Sondheim is the lyricist, and Leonard Bernstein is the composer."

A Kosher Friar

Ever since he made a name for himself as Brother Dominic in television commercials for Xerox copy machines, Jack Eagle has been making personal appearances in his friar's costume. He was at a trade show in the Javits Center, dressed as a monk, when two Hasidim passed by.

"*Oy, iz dos a lebn?*"* Jack sighed.

The Hasidim were startled, then relieved to find that the friar was a Jew.

Jack Eagle

Don't Start Up

When Helen Hayes was guest of honor at a dinner for the Israel Cancer Research Fund, she recalled the time she served as emcee at a dinner where the guest of honor was Arthur Fiedler, the legendary conductor of the Boston Pops.

After the event, Fiedler wrote how honored he was with her presence. Hayes was so "overwhelmed to get this letter" that she wrote back that the honor was all hers. "The letter was very brief but full of passion and sincerity," she said.

A few days later she received another letter: "I didn't mean to start a correspondence.—Arthur Fiedler."

---

* "Is this a life?"

Good Advice

Simcha Dinitz (right) and Henry Kissinger.

Simcha Dinitz, former head of the Jewish Agency and World Zionist Organization, says he can do without speeches.

"Why are we a glutton for punishment—by speaking at all our festivals? Other people sing, dance, eat. We speak!"

What You Say

The late Maurice Blond, a universally beloved insurance executive, once served as chairman of an Israel Bonds luncheon at Whitestone Hebrew Center in Queens, New York. He asked the band to start off with the national anthem.

"How does it go?" asked the bandleader, a new arrival from the Soviet Union.

Maurice started to sing "Oh say..."

"I know it!" the bandleader said and launched into *Osay Shalom.**

---

* Literally, "He who grants peace," a popular liturgical melody.

Getting Better, Thank you

Norm Crosby tells about the time he accompanied Jerry Lewis to a children's hospital. Jerry went around and entertained all the children. There was one kid who sat in a corner and didn't talk. Before he left, Jerry sat down with the kid and sang every song he knew. Then he put his hand on the youngster's shoulder and comforted him: "Kid, I hope you get better."

As he walked out of the room, the kid said, "Jerry, I hope you get better too."

Jerry Lewis

THOMAS VICTOR

Looking for Authenticity

Nothing beats authenticity, if you can find it. You would think to make a movie about Abraham, the father of the Jewish and Arab nations, you would do it in the Holy Land, wouldn't you?

Right. Producers Gerald Rafshoon and Russell Kagan thought of that when they prepared to shoot *Abraham*, the first of a projected series on Biblical heros for Turner Network Television.

They went to Israel to scout locations. What they found was not the land of Abraham, though.

"Too much of the country is highly developed," Rafshoon said. "To get the locations we needed you'd have to move the crews around too many times. There are telephone wires everywhere—even in the desert!"

Rafshoon found all the authentic locations he was looking for in Morocco.

Who Knew?

In his book, *The Jewish Mothers Hall of Fame*, Fred Bernstein interviewed Leah Adler about her son the director, Steve Spielberg.

"When he was growing up," she said, "I didn't know he was a genius. Frankly, I didn't know what the hell he was. For one thing—he'll probably take away my charge accounts for this—Steven was never a good student."

Steven Spielberg

Laugh, Even If It Hurts

Alan King says it is very important to be able to laugh. He tells of his father who went in for an operation. He looked up at the surgeon and said, "Hey, butcher! You better do a good job on me or you'll be in my son's act."

Divine Special Effects

Bernard Jacobs and Gerald Schoenfeld of the Shubert Organization were honored by American Friends of Tel Aviv University. Father George Moore, pastor of St. Malachy's Church, which serves the Broadway community, paid his respects: "When God summoned Moses up the mountain to give him the Ten Commandments, he appeared in brilliant lightning and deafening thunder. As far as I know, that was the earliest use of stage effects."

Life's an Illusion

Mickey Freeman was filming a Delta Airlines commercial in the Garment Center. He was playing a cab driver in the shot. It was in the middle of winter and they took a few breaks to keep warm.

Mickey was sipping coffee behind the wheel of his taxi when a man walked out of the building and looked into the cab, startled at what he saw.

"Mickey, is that you?"

"Yeah, that's me."

"All those years as an actor, you couldn't save any money? Now you have to drive a cab in this weather?"

The man walked away in disgust.

Mickey Freeman

Listen to Mother

Rabbi Arthur Schneier, a Holocaust survivor from Vienna who became the distinguished leader of Park East Synagogue, invoked the memory of his dear mother Gittel, who said, "Some day, Arthur, you will be President."

"Mom," he said, "you have to be born here."

One day he was at the barber when he received an urgent message from his secretary to call his mother right away. She had just learned of John F. Kennedy's assassination and told her son, "Arthur, you must promise me you'll never become President."

Fate Plays a Hand

DIANA MICHENER

Misha Dichter

Cipa and Misha Dichter were destined for each other. World War II forced Misha's parents to flee Warsaw for Shanghai, then to Los Angeles when he was two years old. Cipa's parents escaped from Bialystok and settled in Rio de Janeiro, Brazil. They finally met in New York thirty years ago as students at Juilliard School of Music.

"I looked to my right and saw the most beautiful woman in the school," he recalls. "She looked to her left and saw one of the few men in Juilliard interested in women."

Now tell me there is no *bashert*.*

Not Just Another Movie

It was a dream come true for Holocaust survivor Branko Lustig when he joined his coproducers, Steven Spielberg and Gerald Molen, to accept an Oscar for best film for *Schindler's List*.

Lustig, who had made more than a hundred movies (including *Fiddler on the Roof*) in the last two decades, was especially eager to work on the Schindler project.

First he met with Molen, who produced Spielberg's *Jurassic Park*. Molen, a Christian, asked, "What's your motivation? What drives you to be involved with this film?"

Lustig rolled up his sleeve and showed him his Auschwitz number.

* Destiny, preordained, fated.

Beastly Mail

Actor Ron Perlman, who portrayed the grotesque Vincent character in the title role of the CBS series *Beauty and the Beast*, reported that ninety percent of his mail came from female fans. What in the world can women possibly see in this creature?

"I got letters from women who said they believe they're living with a Vincent."

I asked him to check the mailbag and see if my wife Nina's name is on one of those letters.

Ron Perlman

Can't Take It Anymore

As a kid, James Caan was a terror. In summer camp he was known as Killer Caan. He and his brother went to a rabbi for their bar mitzvah lessons. One day the rabbi called the mother: "If there are two more Jews like your boys, I'm going to become a priest!"

Time to Laugh

Bel Kaufman, author of *Up the Down Staircase*, says her grandfather, Sholom Aleichem, loved the sound of laughter. In fact, he was really ahead of his time because he wrote that laughter is good for your health, which is what doctors today prescribe. "First comes laughter," he wrote. "You can always hang yourself later."

The Donald Honors Honest Abe

Donald Trump said he had not intended to come to Abe Hirschfeld's second seventy-fifth birthday party which Minyan of the Stars sponsored at its Chanukah celebration in 1995 at the Hotel Pennsylvania. (Abe marked his seventy-fifth birthday the year before with New York Governor George Pataki and other celebrities, and decided to do it again.)

"I was in a meeting with twenty-one bloodsucking lawyers," he said. "Abe faxed me his introductory speech. It was eight paragraphs, and seven paragraphs were about me. So I came."

When Hirschfeld introduced his friend, all he said was, "Ladies and gentlemen, Donald Trump will say a few words."

Abe Hirschfeld

Enough Garbage

As mayor of Tel Aviv, Shlomo Lahat would excuse himself from late night parties. He had to go home. He was in the habit of arising at five in the morning, taking a swim, then getting down to business.

During a garbage strike, he was forced to add extra hours to his rigid schedule.

"You work so hard for Tel Aviv," I said. "Maybe you should work for the country—as prime minister?"

"I deal with city garbage, not national garbage," he replied.

Planting a Tree

Sylvia Miles said that fifty years ago she donated twenty-five dollars to plant a tree in Israel.

"I thought that tree would have my name on it," she said.

"When I finally got to Israel, to make a movie, I spent three days looking for my tree. I went to a Jewish National Fund forest and saw thousands of trees. It was the most exciting moment of my life because I realized I had helped establish that forest."

Sylvia Miles

Soap Opera at El Al

El Al president Rafi Harlev's breakfast meeting with the travel press at the airline's New York headquarters turned into a testing ground for a *shidduch.** It started when Gabriel Levenson, travel editor of the New York *Jewish Week*, said he flies El Al to Israel, but frequently stops in London to see his son Tim. His son is a translator who lives outside Paris.

"He's available," Gabriel announced, looking around the room.

"Good," declared Shuly Kustanowitz of *Travel Weekly*. "My daughter Esther is available. She works in the education department at Hadassah in New York."

"Wait a minute!" Harlev chimed in. " I have a son, too!"

---

* A match, an arranged marriage.

Red Buttons (right) with
Leonard Goldstein.

She Can Tell

Red Buttons was in the lobby of the
Concord Hotel when two elderly ladies approached.

"How old are you, Mr. Buttons?"
one asked.

"None of your business!" Red
snapped.

She turned to her friend and said,
"See, I told you he's over seventy."

Negotiating on the Street

Barbra Streisand came to a UJA-Federation dinner honoring her close
friend Steve Ross, head of Time-Warner. She described an experience
that typified the negotiating prowess of the man who headed the world's
biggest media and entertainment conglomerate.

"We were in Corfu, where Steve bargained down a street vendor from
50,000 drachmas to 25,000 drachmas. That's fifty percent down—fifty
percent of $3.98. That's something!"

Praying in God's Language

Neil Simon said that when he was a child, he would accompany his father to *shul*. "It was in a converted store that was so small they needed only three men for a *minyan*," he quipped.

He once tried to read the prayers in English and his father reprimanded him: "Read in Hebrew. God does not understand English."

Neil Simon

Multi-Ethnic Menu

William Gray, a former African-American Congressman from Philadelphia, reports that he occasionally goes to a Jewish function. "I went to a B'nai B'rith affair. They told me they would serve filtered fish. They also said they'll talk *tachlis*.* I didn't know they planned on having Mexican food, too."

Great Jews of the Ages

Harry Belafonte did not know what to say when he addressed American Associates of Ben-Gurion University. "I've come to know that there is nothing you've not heard of—especially from one another."

He reminisced about the glory days when blacks and Jews stood shoulder to shoulder in a unique bond on the march to civil rights.

He was amazed at the vast contributions Jews made to civilization— Marx, Freud, Einstein, "not to mention my friend Buddy Hackett."

* Getting down to business, the bottom line.

Bronx in His Soul

Jan Murray

Jan Murray tells this story about his early years in show business when he set out to improve his image. He got a nose job, fashionable hair style, spiffy new wardrobe, new physique, and an elegant speech. To top it off, he changed his name to suit his new image.

The new, improved Jan Murray was standing in a night club, pleased with his enhanced features. Up came a boyhood pal from the old neighborhood in the Bronx and shouts at the top of his voice, "Murray Janofsky! How are ya?"

Budding Feminist

Elliott Gould is quite proud of his daughter Molly. Even as a child she already had an inquiring mind. "Why do we call it Hebrew?" she once asked. "Why not Shebrew or Webrew?" Obviously, a budding feminist.

It's Enough at Work

Ino Toper came to Israel in 1959 from his native Poland. For seven years he and Nechama Lifshitz were a popular singing duo.

"We were a great couple," he says.

Then why didn't you marry?

"We couldn't live with each other on stage. How could we have survived at home?"

And Then He Made Music

In his book *Findings*, Leonard Bernstein writes that when he was ten years old, he recited the Book of Esther in a Purim play.

"In some very important part of me, I will always be that exiled, frightened little boy of ten, singing the Megillah, and praying for a chance to make music in my lifetime."

Leonard Bernstein

Plain and Fancy

Scott Grauman was three years old and had just come back from his first day at North Shore Hebrew Academy, a day school in Great Neck, Long Island.

"How many kids in your classroom?" asked the proud grandfather, Dr. Ben Futernick.

"Twenty."

"How many teachers do you have?"

"Three. Two Hebrew and one plain."

Alan Dershowitz

Sounds Familiar

Attorney Alan Dershowitz recalls that Yeshiva University refused to admit him due to appallingly dismal grades in Yeshiva High School. Instead, he went to Brooklyn College, then Yale. He presently teaches law at Harvard.

His high school marks were embarrassingly low in Bible, Jewish customs, and behavior.

"The school called my mother in so many times," he says, "everyone thought she worked there."

An Illusion

Shari Lewis' father, Dr. Abraham Hurwitz, was a professor at Yeshiva University. At one time he was appointed by Mayor Fiorello LaGuardia as official magician of New York. In his classes, where he taught methods of education, he would conjure up all his skills at magic to emphasize a point.

To illustrate how creative her father was, Shari relates an encounter with Eleanor Roosevelt. Her father happened to be in a playground when Mrs. Roosevelt passed by. She stopped and asked him to perform a trick. At the moment, he had nothing with him by way of magic equipment.

What to do? He made a dollar bill move across the table.

How did he do it? Mrs. Roosevelt did not notice, but Hurwitz put a piece of chewing gum on the back of a cockroach and stuck the dollar bill on its back.

Food for Everyone Else

George Burns recalled growing up in a slum tenement on the Lower East Side where his family was very poor. His father Leo was a *mashgiach*.*

"He made sure that everybody on the Lower East Side had kosher food," George said. "Anybody had a wedding, a bar mitzvah, like that, he went to see that the food was kosher. Everybody had kosher food and we had nothing to eat."

George Burns

That's Marriage

Arnold Forster, the distinguished counsel of the Anti-Defamation League, was persuaded by his wife, May, to address Elem, an organization that helps distressed youth in Israel.

"Do I really have to make a speech?" Arnold protested.

May said it was important that he come to the luncheon because she was to be the guest of honor.

"I'm not a henpecked husband," Arnold insisted. "I'm going to prove it by coming, but I'm not going to make a speech. All I'm going to say is I love you."

At the affair, Arnold recited a story about a man going to heaven. There were two gates. One was marked HENPECKED HUSBANDS and had a long line. The other was marked NON-HENPECKED HUSBANDS and no one in line. He stood at the non-henpecked gate. He was the only one.

"What are you doing at this gate?" the angel asked.

"I don't know," the man said. "My wife told me to stand here."

---

* Kashrut inspector, who attests to the kosher status of the food that is prepared and served.

Still Searching for Matzah

Howie Mandel

Wacky comedian Howie Mandel always followed his own path. He got kicked out of Hebrew school in Toronto. His parents brought in a private tutor for his bar mitzvah.

"I got a lot of envelopes—mostly empty!"

His parents would have been thrilled if he had gone to medical school. But he was a high school dropout. Nevertheless he became a doctor in spite of it all—he played Dr. Wayne Fiscus for six years on TV's *St. Elsewhere.*

Howie lives in Los Angeles with his wife, Terry, and three children. They belong to a Conservative synagogue and enjoy the holidays, especially Passover.

"My six-year-old Alex is still looking for the *afikomen.** I hid it real good this year."

It's How You Dress

Business consultant and Israel Bonds leader Howard Samuels was standing outside the Regency Hotel on the East Side when a tattered beggar approached. The character stopped, took one look at Samuels, then reached in his pocket and gave him a quarter.

"You know how bad I looked!" Samuels chuckled.

"Did you take the quarter?" I asked.

"Yes. I think I'll go back tomorrow."

---

* From the Greek, meaning "dessert." A piece of matza set aside during the early part of the Passover *Seder* to be distributed and eaten at the end of the meal. Children try to find it and hold it for ransom.

Songwriter's Backup

Anthony Newley, who writes many of his songs, told the Concord Hotel crowd how he wrote *Wouldn't That Be Nice*. First he wrote a poem. Then he asked Burt Bacharach if he would like to put it to music. Nothing happened.

"So I went to Marvin Hamlisch," Newley related, "and said I have a second-hand poem. In two days he made a song out of it. Goes to show you, if you write a song with Burt Bacharach, you better have Marvin Hamlisch's phone number."

Marvin Hamlisch

Budding Critic

When *Kramer vs. Kramer* came out, Dustin Hoffman took his nine-year-old Jenna to see his film. He asked her what age group the movie would appeal to. "Anybody would love it," the kid said. "But I wouldn't show it to anyone under nine."

Not PC to Be Jewish

It took Jackie Mason thirty years to become an overnight hit on Broadway. He could have become a television sensation sooner, but all the Jewish producers and agents were fearful that he was "too Jewish."

"Why that should be I don't know," Jackie says. "No one ever told Bill Cosby he's too *shvartz*.*"

---

* Black.

Jay Leno (left) and Marvin Silbermintz.

Making Jay Leno Laugh

A dozen years ago, a thirty-nine-year-old comedy writer watched Jay Leno perform on David Letterman's television show. "I saw the best comedian of our time," Marvin Silbermintz told his wife. He called Leno to see if he could use an aspiring—or perspiring—writer. Leno invited Marvin to work on an ABC-TV special.

"Jay," Marvin said, "I don't work Friday nights. I'm an observant Jew."

"Don't worry about it," Leno said.

Marvin accompanied the comedian to Harrah's in Reno. It was his first time in a casino. And he was wearing his *yarmulke* as he always did.

"Maybe I should wear a cap," he asked timidly, not looking to embarrass the comedian who was starring in the hotel's showroom.

"No," Leno said emphatically. "Why should you hide what you are?"

So Marvin began a career of writing comedy for one of the most popular and talented comedians of our time. Wherever he travels with Leno, he takes his *tefilin** and drops into the local synagogue.

It is not surprising that Marvin, an Orthodox young man, should be writing gags for Leno. The Bronx native did magic tricks at age eleven at Samson Raphael Hirsch Yeshiva in the Washington Heights section of upper Manhattan. He was a hit in the annual Chanukah show.

"Those rebbes were tough," he remembers. "If I told a joke and made people laugh in Talmud class, I'd get a *potch*.**"

Today, when he writes a joke that makes Leno laugh, he gets a check.

* Small black boxes mounted on leather straps, worn on the arm and on the head by Jews at weekday morning prayers. Biblical verses, handwritten on parchment, are enclosed in each box.
** Slap.

Secret of a Happy Relationship

Kirk Douglas and Burt Lancaster were the best of friends for ages. Hal Wallis asked how they got along so well, and Kirk answered, "Burt talks about himself, I talk about myself, and neither of us listens to the other."

Kirk Douglas

It's Too Good

Chaim Harari, president of Weizmann Institute of Science, got a phone call at his Rehovot office.

"Hello, Chaim, how is everything at the institute?"

"Everything is going extremely well."

"Oh, you are sitting with visitors. I'll call you later."

Hasidim and Yoga

Peter Max is very high on yoga. It is something the pop artist recommends to everybody. "Yoga is not a religion," he says. "It's strictly a science. It will make a Jew a better Jew. It will make a Christian a better Christian. The whole idea—the stretching, the eating, the vegetarianism — is to find inner peace and to create a strong body from the postures."

He would recommend it especially to Hasidim because "as much they are the most fabulous guys in the world—keeping the whole Jewish aspect alive—the Jewish diet isn't the greatest. It has very high cholesterol. You go to some of the doctors and you see only Hasidim sitting there."

Schnorring for Good Cause

TIM BOXER

Yitzhak Rabin

At the annual dinner of American Committee for Shaare Zedek Medical Center, dinner chairman Menno Ratzker told of meeting the late Yitzhak Rabin in Washington.

"Did you know Ludwig Jesselson?" Ratzker asked about one of the founders of the Jerusalem hospital.

"Of course I did," Rabin said. "He used to shlep me around the United States to schnorr for Shaare Zedek."

Fun While It Lasted

At an Israel Cancer Research Fund dinner, trustee Gloria Wang said her husband, Sam Wang, was a founder of Kiryat Arba in Israel and operated a fleet of tankers before he succumbed to colon cancer. She attended a cocktail party where a gentleman bored his listeners about his newly acquired yacht.

"Did your husband ever own a yacht?" he asked.

"He never cared much for little boats," she replied.

During World War II, Wang registered at a Cairo hotel where they ushered him into their most luxurious suite. In the middle of the night they knocked on the door and threw him out.

"From his name," Gloria said, "they thought he was the ambassador from China—till the real ambassador came."

Talmud Helps

Investment manager Jack Nash was visiting an executive training firm in Tokyo. He was surprised to see three volumes of the Steinsaltz Talmud translated into Japanese. What in the world would a Japanese company want with the Talmud?

"They said they deal with Hasidim in the diamond business," Jack said. "The Japanese wanted to study the Talmud to glean some insight into negotiating with the Hasidim."

A Natural Actor

Rabbi Marc Schneier of the Hamptons Synagogue faced the hazards of a film "fire" only to plunge into the path of Long Island's burning brush of the summer of '95. He survived the perils of both.

Schneier expected that his acting debut in a movie titled, appropriately enough, *The Substance of Fire*, would trigger high anxiety. But he was quite cool about the experience. In fact, it was a role made for him.

The movie was shot in New York with Sarah Jessica Parker, Ron Rifkin, and Timothy Hutton in the lead roles. It is about a Jewish family in Bronx that deals with a crisis in the family business.

Schneier officiates at a graveside scene. He eulogizes the character played by Hutton.

"They did not have to give me any coaching," the rabbi reported. "Parker said I was a natural for the role."

Joy of Living

Tony Curtis, who says "We must never lose the joy of living," set a prime example when he arrived in New York to preside over the Emanuel Foundation's 1995 dinner. He is honorary chairman of the organization, named in memory of his father, which promotes the welfare of the Jewish community in Budapest, Hungary. The event honored the memory of Madeleine Herling who, with her husband, the philanthropist Erwin Herling, established a Victims Memorial Tree in Budapest.

Tony was accompanied by a tall, buxom blonde straight out of Central Casting, by the name of Jill Vandenberg, a horseback riding instructor in San Diego.

I raised my eyes and gazed on a white satin gown that was cut front and aft so low as to reveal almost all of Jill's assets, which defied Newton's law of gravity. Her shoes enabled her to tower above the admiring crowd at the lofty height of six feet, two inches.

Dr. Norman Lamm, president of Yeshiva University, was amused: "It's interesting to see how everyone's trying to get close to her—the women out of envy and the men out of jealousy."

TIM BOXER

Tony Curtis

Peace Above All

What does "peace at any price" mean? To Shimon Peres it might mean one thing, but to Rona Jaffe's father it meant something else.

Samuel Jaffe was Orthodox; his wife, Diana, Conservative. When Samuel asked Moses Ginsberg for his daughter's hand, he was told, "You know, Diana has some very strong ideas on things and you're going to have to give in."

"In my father's family," says the author of thirteen novels, "they were Sephardic and Orthodox. They were brought up with peace at any price. Peace in the family was the most important thing. So he wasn't Orthodox anymore."

Rona Jaffe

Take It Easy

Preparing for a tour in Florida, singer Ron Eliran called his friend in Miami, a renowned cantor.

"May I use your sound system?" Ron asked. "I don't want to shlep mine around. I'm afraid of getting a hernia."

"Funny you should say that," his friend replied. "I just had an operation."

"What happened?"

"I won first place in a *shofar*-blowing contest. I blew the last sound so long I got a hernia."

But They Understood

Oscar Brand

Oscar Brand said his father was fourteen when he came from England to settle in Manitoba. He was hired by the Hudson Bay Company to interpret to the Indians.

"He couldn't speak Indian," Oscar said, "but the Indians couldn't tell that to the Hudson Bay Company except through him."

Now That's a Car!

When he was a celebrated baseball coach, Billy Martin pulled up to the Stage Delicatessen in a swanky limousine. He proudly announced that the car cost one hundred thousand dollars.

"You should hear the sound system!" he exclaimed.

"For one hundred thousand dollars," owner Lou Auerbach cracked, "you should have Ray Charles playing."

Respect, Please, for Holy Disease

Matthew Nargo, a former vice president of CBS Broadcast Group, reminds us of a time when many New Yorkers had little knowledge of Jews.

The police examination had a question: "What are rabies and how do you treat them?"

One candidate wrote: "Rabies are Jewish priests and I treat them with respect."

Don't Call Him by His Name

David Fisher, the Israeli singing sensation who starred in *Les Miserables* on Broadway, is universally known as Dudu. Recently he became sensitive about his nickname.

"In Israel, Europe and South Africa, I'm Dudu and that's okay. But in America, I don't want to be called Dudu. I just found out it's a four-letter word."

David "Dudu" Fisher
(center) with
Nina and Tim Boxer.

Tools for the Mind

Comedian-actor David Brenner is dissecting the stereotypical Jewish mother. What he cannot understand is why Jewish mothers do not permit their little boys to play with tools.

"They take your hammer away: 'Bad hammer! Bad hammer! Here, take a book, book, book!'"

When he grew up, David says, he always knocked a nail in the wall . . . with a book.

Praying with Alef-Bet

*André Gregory (left) and
Rabbi Ephraim Buchwald.*

André Gregory, star of Louis Malle's 1981 classic film, *My Dinner with André*, was born Jewish in Paris, baptized Russian Orthodox in New York at age thirteen, turned Episcopalian at age twenty-three, and lately has come out of the closet as a proud Jew. That is due in large measure to his friendship with Rabbi Ephraim Buchwald, founder of the National Jewish Outreach Project (NJOP) and leader of the popular Beginner's Service at Lincoln Square Synagogue in New York.

"Effie's call to come home," Andre said at NJOP's second annual dinner, "reverberated in my head. I suddenly got this urge to come home to Judaism. He started me on my *alef-bet*."

On a trip to Lithuania to see where his father came from, Andre found only a deserted graveyard in the forest. "I wanted to say a prayer," he said. "I just stood there and read Effie's book. I said the *alef-bet*."

He found himself in Norway on the High Holidays. He wanted to go to a synagogue, but was stopped by security. The fear of terrorists was in the air.

He showed his passport. They said Gregory is not a Jewish name.

He told them about attending the Beginner's Service at Lincoln Square Synagogue and studying with Effie Buchwald. They let him in.

Carry on for Dad

Hal Linden, who starred in the *Barney Miller* television show for eight years, received countless requests to appear at fund-raising events and charity affairs. But he had very little time to make such personal appearances.

One such letter, though, aroused his curiosity. It was from Bnai Zion, asking for his help to raise money to build a rehabilitation center for disabled war veterans in Israel.

"I stopped in my tracks," he recalled. "My father, Charles Lipschitz, who came from Keidan, Lithuania, was a founding member of Bnai Zion. I remember as a kid there were meetings at our house, or Dad wouldn't be home because he's at a Bnai Zion meeting."

Hal responded, and now there is a plaque dedicated to the memory of his father at Beth Halochem in Haifa.

Hal Linden

TIM BOXER

Sabbath Rituals

Manny Saks, a former RCA Records talent coordinator and discoverer of such talents as Frank Sinatra and Dinah Shore, was thought to be Orthodox. He would leave the office in New York every Friday afternoon and go home to his mother in Philadelphia. She would light the Sabbath candles.

His friends did not know, till after his death, that every Saturday morning he would go into a hospital and have his blood changed. He had leukemia.

Praying in the Strangest Places

Mark Weiner

Marc Weiner, the Orthodox comedian who hosts *Weinerville* on Nickelodeon cable, runs a family business producing laughs. His father, Mel, is his business adviser. Mother Adelle runs the merchandising end. When Marc hits the road with his comedy show, mom's in the lobby pushing Weinerville items, such as T-shirts, posters, and puppet stuff. Wife, Sandy, helps write some of the funny lines.

"Don't Orthodox people say a prayer after using the bathroom?" Sandy asked.

"Yes," Marc said. "Don't you?"

"I pray that no one goes in there when I come out."

Good Question

"For us Jews," Dr. Ruth Westheimer told the ladies of the Nassau region of Hadassah on Long Island, "sex has never been considered a sin. In the marriage ceremony a man promises three things: food, shelter, and sexual gratification."

When she hosted her NBC radio program, a man called in with a question. He'd been living with a woman for a year and was now getting ready to marry her. What could he do on his wedding night to make it different from all previous nights?

"After the ceremony, after you've counted all the checks," the sex therapist advised, "go into the bathroom. When you come out, do not be in pajamas. Wear only a tie and a top hat."

"Where should I put the top hat?" he asked.

Learning to Be Jewish

Barbara Carrera, the international-model-turned-actress, a beauty from Nicaragua, knew nothing of Jewish culture until she went to Israel to star in an NBC television movie, *Masada*.

To learn more about the country, she decided against staying at the Tel Aviv Sheraton. Instead she took an apartment in gritty Jaffa to be close to the artists. Then she moved into a villa in Arad, near Masada.

"The neighbors in Arad invited me to a traditional Rosh Hashanah feast. They kept saying, 'Eat, Barbara, eat.' Reminded me of Grossinger's."

Barbara Carrera

Taking Care of Chuckenyu

Representative Charles Schumer of Queens, New York, was in his freshman year on Capitol Hill when his grandmother buttonholed Speaker of the House Tip O'Neill and proceeded to relate her life story.

"I had three sons," she said. "They all served in the war. None ran away, because they were breastfed."

She ended her conversation with "Take good care of Chuckenyu."

Next day Schumer was summoned by O'Neill. You do not get called by the Speaker unless you have displeased him. Understandably, Schumer was quite nervous as he entered the office.

"Charles," O'Neill said, "your grandmother is a very fine woman. I loved hearing her life story. But tell me, what's a chuckenyu and how do we take care of it?"

Nell Carter

The Valley of Death

A couple of years ago, Nell Carter was at death's door. She suffered a brain aneurysm and was in a Los Angeles hospital. "Your brain bursts and you start bleeding," she explains.

This was the extraordinary singer who electrified Broadway in *Ain't Misbehavin'* and received a Tony Award for it. She went on to star for six years in her own television series, *Gimme a Break*.

Now she was on her deathbed. She remembers saying, "Okay, God, whatever you want."

Being Jewish — having converted from Presbyterianism to Judaism ten years before — she asked for a *siddur*.* "I tried to read the Twenty-third Psalm, and I felt calm," Nell recalls. "I decided to read and pray to God as I know him. Religion is very beautiful."

Nell made it through her ordeal. Others with the same problem are not so lucky, she realizes. Her survival could mean only one thing: God loves her.

Mind Your Manners

Harmonica genius Larry Adler toured Africa in 1943 with Jack Benny. In Marrakech they were invited to the sultan's palace.

It took eight men on both sides to push open the gigantic doors.

"Now, Jack," Larry quipped, "mind your manners. Don't slam the door."

* Hebrew Prayerbook.

Jewish Connection

Some think Michael Caine is Jewish. Not so, but he does have a Jewish connection. He was baptized in the Church of England as Morris Joseph Micklewhite, but the fact that he was educated at a private Jewish school in London adds to the widespread impression that he is a Jew.

"I was one of twelve Protestants in the entire school," he said. "It was the Hackney Downs Grammar School. We were a rough lot, and in the end I got thrown out. I went to another school. I wasn't happy at school. But I can carry on a conversation in Yiddish."

Michael Caine

He said his father was Catholic and his mother Protestant, and his wife, Shakira, is Muslim.

"Bob Hope once said that I wasn't sure there was a God, but if there were, I didn't want to lose out on a technicality."

Worthy Qualities

At the Park East Synagogue's 105th annual dinner in Manhattan, president Michael Scharf told a story about board chairman Julius Gewirtz's grandson.

The kid wrote a school essay on the three greatest men: Moses, George Washington, and his grandfather Julius.

"Why did you include your grandfather?" the teacher asked.

"Because," the child said, "he helps poor people, supports schools around the world, and is the kindest person I know."

Bilko and the Bookies

Mickey Freeman, who played Private Fielding Zimmerman on *The Phil Silvers Show* in the 1950s, does lectures about those halcyon days of television. He is often asked if Sergeant Bilko really was a gambler. He answers with a story about the time he was booked at a United Way fundraiser in Toronto. The audience consisted of fifty bookmakers. As he stepped on stage, they gave him a standing ovation.

"Wait a minute," Mickey said. "I haven't done anything yet."

They said they weren't applauding for him. It was for Phil Silvers.

"He sent my wife to Europe," said one bookie.

"He paid for my house."

"He sent my kid to college."

It turned out that when Silvers worked burlesque, he would stay six months in Toronto. He would gamble, mostly without success, on baseball, basketball, and horses. The bookies would come to the box office and say, "We need his salary." He lost $125,000 in a month.

The appreciative bookies came to the United Way dinner and contributed vast sums to the charity—in cash.

Mickey Freeman as Private Zimmerman.

Can't be too Careful

A suitcase was spotted in a corner of the Grand Ballroom of the New York Hilton during a Bnai Zion dinner. It looked suspicious to executive vice president Mel Parness. Scores of bomb squad officers with a couple of sniffing dogs responded to his alarm. As the eight hundred black-tie guests poured down the escalators, one gentleman calmly reached for the suitcase, which he had not had time to check in the coat room, and joined the evacuation.

Doing the Right Thing,
No Matter What

Mike Burstyn is not your typical showbiz Sammy Glick who'd do anything to succeed.

When his movie, *Kuni Leml*, was named the official Israeli entry at the 1967 Moscow Film Festival, Mike was overjoyed. That was a prestigious career step for him.

It so happened that the Six-Day War broke out on the festival's opening day. That was not good timing. Instead of attending the gala ceremonies and meeting with the world's major film folk, Mike was in uniform entertaining the troops on the battlefields of the Negev.

"It was a big blow to miss the film festival," he says. "But my first priority was the safety of my people."

A dozen years later, the singer-actor again was set to visit the Soviet Union. This time he would represent the Committee for Russian Jewry, based in London.

Mike Burstyn

"It was *Simchat Torah*,*" he recalls. "I was going to perform for the Jews of Moscow on the street outside the synagogue."

Again it was not to be.

His mother-in-law was dying of cancer in New York. Mike looked at her face, and her eyes begged him, "Please don't leave. Stay with Edie and the children. They need you now."

"It was a difficult decision," Mike recalls. "But I didn't hesitate. I told her I'm staying. She was so relieved. It added days to her life."

---

* Literally, "Rejoicing in the Law." The festival after Sukkot marking both the completion and the beginning of the annual cycle of Torah readings in the synagogue.

It All Depends

Sammy Shore

Sammy Shore grew up in Chicago, where his father had a used furniture store. Above the store he ran a rooming house. There were three-dollar rooms, four-dollar rooms, and five-dollar rooms.

The rooms were all the same. It all depended on whether you had three dollars, four dollars, or five dollars.

How to Make It, How to Save It

Comedian Dan Curtis reports that when his daughter, Jennie, went with her husband, Bill, on their first trip to Las Vegas, they scurried straight to the slot machines. They dropped seven quarters in the slots—and out came five thousand dollars.

"She called to tell me the news that she won five thousand dollars," Dan said, "and she called collect."

Surprise

Art D'Lugoff, who ran the Village Gate, learned Hebrew at Yeshiva of Flatbush in Brooklyn.

In conversation with a couple of Israelis at his Greenwich Village nightspot, Art used Hebrew with ease.

The Israelis were surprised. "You understand Hebrew?" they asked.

"No," Art said. "I only speak it."

Waiting for Abby

I met Melissa Gilbert at a Chabad rehabilitation home for Jewish women in Culver City, California. Melissa, who played Laura Ingalls Wilder for nine years on NBC's *Little House on the Prairie*, was waiting for a twenty-six-year-old Jewish woman named Abby, a drug addict. They had a date to film a segment for the annual Chabad telethon.

Abby never showed up, so Melissa filmed the segment herself, expressing her profound feelings for the troubled Jewish druggies roaming the streets of Los Angeles.

Melissa Gilbert and Rabbi Shlomo Cunin.

"The best kind of love I know is Jewish love," Melissa said. "I was brought up by it. I was enveloped by it, and taught and nurtured by a loving, giving, closely knit, supportive Jewish family."

Vat Is Dat?

When tourists leave Israel with gifts they purchased, they may exchange their VAT (Value Added Tax) receipts for refunds.

"You know why they call it VAT?" says Leon Charash, a full-time pediatric neurosurgeon and part-time wit of Woodbury, New York.

"You ask for your money back and they say, 'Vat?'"

Loyal to the End

Ed Koch

As a Congressman, Ed Koch was invited to the regular prayer breakfast in Congress to speak about Judaism.

"I didn't know much," he said. "I called my rabbi, and I went to the Library of Congress. I came armed with a lot of exotic facts. I spoke about *kashrut*, the three branches of Judaism. Then came the question period. There was only one question: Do Jews have dual loyalty?"

Koch told his fellow Congressmen: "You never ask that if one comes from Italy, Ireland, Greece. But you do ask it of Jews."

He raised his hand and declared: "I solemnly swear that if Israel ever invades the United States, I shall stand with the United States."

Not What She Seems

Fran Drescher, who plays the ultimate Jewish American Princess on TV's *Nanny*, was always typecast as a princess.

The 1977 Miss New York Teenager made her film debut as an Italian American Princess in *Saturday Night Fever*.

Then Terry Leibling, Marvin Hamlisch's sister, a casting agent, was searching for a Jewish American Princess for the film *American Hot Wax*. She auditioned Fran and proclaimed her to be the perfect JAP for the role.

Fran disclaims the princess title. "If I were a JAP," she says, "I wouldn't be married to an actor—it would be a doctor!"

Resorting to Extreme Measures

Myron Cohen lived in New City, New York, next to Temple Beth Sholom. When there was a bar mitzvah or wedding, the overflow of cars were parked in Myron's driveway. Sometimes he could not get his own car out.

This went on until an exasperated Myron called the rabbi and told him, "If you don't straighten out this parking problem, I'm going to become a Catholic."

Myron Cohen

Seeking the Right Solution

Simon Cohen, the senior rabbi at the Concord Resort Hotel, has to cope with myriad details on every holiday. He says a Jew finds a solution for every problem. If you were told you had an incurable disease, how would you react? It depends on who you are, Simon says.

The Catholic: "I'd go to confession and do charitable work till the end of my days."

The Protestant: "In the morning I'd go to church and at night I'd paint the town red."

The Jew: "I'd get a second opinion."

Future in Good Hands

Following a bus explosion in Jerusalem by a Hamas suicide bomber in February 1996, Israeli Chief Rabbi Yisroel Meir Lau made the requisite condolence calls. He came to the home of a young couple who were among the victims of the terrorist attack. The Russian immigrant couple lived in a poor section of the city. They left in their home two little boys—Vladek, who was eight years old, and a sabra, Tomer, six months old.

The woman also left a sister by the name of Larissa. She was recently married and had no children yet.

Lau sat on the couch with Vladek. The youngster knew full well the tragic situation. In fact, he was promising everybody that he would take care of his younger brother.

"Vladek," his aunt said, "do you know who came to visit us? The chief rabbi of Israel!" She spoke in Russian.

"The chief rabbi made *aliyah* at your age, when he was eight, also without a father and mother. You see, even being an orphan, so young, he became the chief rabbi of our state. So don't lose hope, Vladek. If you want, your future is in your hands."

Iraeli Chief Rabbi Yisroel Meir Lau

TIM BOXER

Honoring a Master Artist

Aaron Copland, who got an Academy Award for his music in *The Heiress* and the Pulitzer Prize for his ballet *Appalachian Spring*, was given a creative arts award at the Hebrew Arts School in New York.

Victor Borge, the guest artist, bounded on stage and announced, "Master Copland, I will honor you by *not* playing the piano."

Victor Borge

Rabbi had Timing

Comedian-singer-radio star Harry Richman made a trans atlantic flight in 1938, and prayers were said for a safe journey at Ezrath Israel Temple in the heart of Broadway.

In the synagogue's yearbook, Richman wrote, "It is a real pleasure to know that no matter how busy we are, the little *shul* always finds time to think of and be helpful to us."

The "little *shul*" was known far and wide as the Actors Temple. Members included Oscar Levant, Milton Berle, Eddie Cantor, Jack Benny, and numerous other celebrities.

Ann Birstein, daughter of the late spiritual leader of the temple, Rabbi Bernard Birstein, wrote a book, *The Rabbi on 47th Street*, chronicling the story of this unique house of worship that served show biz Jews.

"The actors didn't mind that it was an Orthodox synagogue," Ann told me. "In fact they wanted it to be like their parents had."

Red Buttons told Ann that the crowd at Lindy's always looked forward to the High Holidays and the rabbi's sermons. "He was our kind of rabbi—he had timing."

No Ticket, No Show

When Mordecai Ben-David performed at a concert in Tel Aviv, security was so tight that the guard at the stage door would not let him in.

"Show me your ticket," the guard demanded.

"He's the performer!" the people shouted.

"I don't care who he is," the guard insisted. "If he doesn't have a ticket, he doesn't get in."

That's Life!

Marc Daniels, a veteran Hollywood director (among whose credits is TV's *Alice*, which starred Linda Lavin), remembers when he did *Arsenic and Old Lace* on live television in the early days of the tube.

"An actor was supposed to open a window box and find a corpse. We rehearsed it and then shot it. The actor went over to the window, opened the box, and the corpse, played by an extra, opened his eyes. We couldn't reshoot, it was live television, so the audience saw a corpse with blinking eyes."

Most Important Thing in a Career

Kirk Douglas, speaking at a drama school, was asked by a student, "What medium—television, stage, film—would be most fulfilling to me as an actress?"

His answer: "Just get a job."

Eager to Learn

Joey Bishop married a Catholic woman named Sylvia Ruzga. Once he came home and she wasn't there. He looked everywhere for her. He finally found her at the synagogue—in a class on how to make a Passover *Seder*.

Joey Bishop

You Can Count on Him

Appearances to the contrary, Israel's former ambassador to the United Nations, Yoram Aridor, had a unique sense of humor. At a party at Bnai Zion, welcoming him to the post, he said that he was asked in the Knesset, "What can you promise us at the United Nations?"

He thought for a moment. "I can promise you one thing," he replied. "My vote will always be for Israel."

Showing Respect

Geraldo Rivera

Geraldo Rivera's Jewish mother wanted her son to have a religious identity, so the family joined the newly established Temple Beth El on Long Island. The synagogue was too small to hold his bar mitzvah, so Geraldo celebrated at the North Lindenhurst Volunteer Fire Department.

In his autobiography, *Exposing Myself*, Geraldo says the rabbi called on him to read in Hebrew from the Torah at the makeshift podium. Recognizing the solemnity of the moment, everyone fell silent. The audience on the father's side was a Puerto Rican crowd.

"As I began to read," Geraldo writes, "the assembled Rivera clan, unfamiliar with Jewish ritual, but wanting to acknowledge the moment with appropriate respect, removed their *yarmulkes* and placed the skullcaps over their hearts."

Cash and Carry

Danny Levine welcomed a customer at his J. Levine Bookstore in Manhattan: "I'm Levine. May I help you?"

"I'm Cash," the man said.

"We also take credit cards," Levine said.

"I'm Cash—Johnny Cash."

The singing star bought the Book of Ruth. He said a woman friend, a convert to Judaism, was getting married and asked him to read a selection from the book.

Incidentally, Cash paid cash.

Knocking Out the Missiles

The devotion of a Quaker's daughter helped save Israel's air force from annihilation by Syria's Soviet-made SAM missiles in the 1982 Lebanon campaign.

I learned this piece of history at a Technion-Israel Institute of Technology dinner where one of the guests was Joan Goldberg Arbuse, the eighty-four-year-old former aviatrix and race horse breeder. She said her mother was a Quaker, her father a Jew. Her mother, who was expelled from the Society of Friends because her brief acting career shocked the Elders, instilled in her daughter the paramount importance of *chesed*.* Her mother did work for the Hebrew Sheltering Guardian Orphan Asylum in Pleasantville, New York, and made Joan work there, too.

One of the boys in the orphanage, Isidor Goldberg, became a test pilot, then an electronics pioneer, and in 1919 the founder of Pilot Radio Corporation which, for fifty years, was the largest producer of short-wave radio transmitters and receivers. In 1923 he bought land in Haifa and donated it to the five-year-old Technion for a new building. In 1936 he married Joan, the girl who had given so much of her time taking care of the orphanage.

After her husband's death in 1961, Joan established the Isidor Goldberg Electronics Center at Technion.

In 1973, Russian-developed anti-aircraft missiles deployed in Egypt and Syria destroyed fifty Israeli planes in the first three days of the Yom Kippur War. Israel suffered devastating losses from those missiles, which played a dominant role in the war.

were poised in the Bekaa Valley.

In a confidential letter to Joan, Moshe Pearlman, a Technion official, described how Israeli pilots used newly developed scientific instruments

---

* Favor, grace, benevolence (charitable work).

"to discover the frequencies on which the SAMs operate, and neutralize them with our own electronically guided countermissiles riding the same radar beam used by the Soviet missile radar to seek out our own aircraft."

With a combination of electronic ingenuity and brilliant aerial tactics, Israeli pilots succeeded in knocking out all nineteen batteries of SAM missiles in an incredible two-and-a-half hours—without the loss of a single plane. This was due mainly to the scientific creativity of the Isidor Goldberg Electronic Center at Technion, the research school that Joan had founded in her husband's memory.

"We achieved a revolutionary technological breakthrough of crucial interest to military staffs throughout the world," Pearlman wrote. "The Kremlin must be gravely concerned, and the Pentagon happy."

TIM BOXER

Benjamin Netanyahu

What's Going On?

When Benjamin Netanyahu was Ambassador to the United Nations, he made a visit to Rome. He noticed a lot of police activity around his hotel. "What's going on?" he asked.

"Oh, don't you know?" a police officer said. "We have the Israeli Ambassador to the United Nations staying here."

Keeping Time with Faith

Polly Bergen calls herself the only Jewish Southern Baptist in the country.

She was born in Knoxville, where her maternal grandfather was a Baptist minister. She credits her interest in Judaism to her former husband, agent Freddie Fields. His family belonged to a Reform temple in Flushing, Queens.

"The more I was exposed to his faith," she said, "the more I was convinced that it was a religion that made sense to me."

Freddie's rabbi converted her in 1956. It was strictly her own decision, no suggestion of it from Freddie.

"You know what they say—converts are more devoted than the native born. I always had to remind everybody when it was the High Holidays."

Polly Bergen

Upstaging the Star

Gene Barry was the star of *Bat Masterson* and *The Name of the Game* on television. His first professional job was in a Yiddish play with Menasha Skulnick at the Second Avenue Theater. He was six feet, one inch, too tall and too slim to fit into the soldier's uniform they wore. The sleeves came up to his elbow; the pants came up to his knees.

"I was getting laughs and Skulnick was getting jealous," Barry remembers. "I almost got fired."

Singing for His Supper

It was 1944, when Scotch was impossible to come by. Bing Crosby and Louis B. Mayer dropped into the renowned Lower East Side restaurant Moskowitz & Lupowitz.

Louis Anzelowitz, always the gracious host, asked if they wanted anything special. Bing, who well knew it was unattainable, asked for a Scotch.

"What kind?" Louis asked.

Bing smiled. "Martin's."

"What age?"

Bing frowned. "Are you putting me on?"

"If I'm putting you on, I'd be in Hollywood."

Bing, going along with what he believed was an innocent game, said, "Twenty years old."

"With the brass bird on the chain around the bottle?"

Anzelowitz ran up three flights to a secret storeroom where he kept a huge supply of liquor from before the war. He returned triumphantly with the very bottle in question.

He summoned a violinist and told Crosby, "Here it is. Just sing one chorus of your favorite song for my customers and it's yours."

That's how Bing Crosby came to sing *Melancholy Baby* at Moskowitz & Lupowitz.

His Favorite Song

Roberta Peters was in Israel just before the Six-Day War broke out. She was touring with Richard Tucker and the Israel Philharmonic Orchestra. She was puzzled by the disappearance of several members of the orchestra until she found out that they were assembling in the forests, getting into their tanks.

She stayed during the war and entertained the troops. She stood on a makeshift platform in the Negev and sang for three thousand airmen and -women.

As she was leaving the base, a soldier shouted, "You didn't sing my favorite song!"

"What is it?"

"*Chicago.* That's where I'm from."

Roberta Peters

Could Be a Halo

Representative Charles Schumer took a stroll in Forest Hills, Queens, to meet his constituents.

"Mr. Schumer," one woman said, "you have more courage than anyone else in Congress. I watch you on C-Span, and I always see you with a *yarmulke.*"

"It's not a *yarmulke,*" Schumer responded as he bent over to show his bald spot.

Victor Borge

Needs His Own Piano

Victor Borge told his wife, Sanna, as they dashed to the airport for a trip to Toronto, that he wished he'd brought his piano.

She assured him there would be a piano there.

"I wish I'd brought my own piano."

"Why?"

"Because I left the airline tickets on it."

The Only Cure

Dr. Rick Berenstein had a noisy parakeet in his Manhattan apartment. It was driving him crazy.

"You are a psychoanalyst," I said. "Can't you do anything to cure that bird?"

"I did," he said. "I looked that bird in the eye and said, 'Does thirty seconds in the microwave mean anything to you?'"

Getting a Jump-Start in Life

David "Dudu" Fisher was a bit apprehensive when he applied for the cantor's position at the Great Synagogue in Tel Aviv. After all, at twenty-one years of age, he was considered too young. Too, he was cleanshaven, not properly religious, and he was not married. In other words, this was one candidate totally unsuited for such a lofty position at this Orthodox *shul*.

As luck would have it, his uncle, Rabbi Shalom Merkin, had connections. Merkin interceded with the synagogue authorities, prevailing upon them to hire his nephew. The bargaining chip was that they need not pay him one shekel. The uncle, wealthy from real estate holdings, would provide the synagogue with his nephew's salary.

Of course, Dudu had no inkling of this secret deal. He accepted the offer from the synagogue and was happy with the fee. The uncle was glad to help his nephew, fresh out of the army, get established in his profession.

After one year, Dudu took a similar position in Netanya at double the salary. His career was taking off. He gave concerts abroad. He starred in the Tel Aviv production of *Les Miserables* and then made his Broadway debut in the same show.

How Much Quieter?

Molly Picon once gave little Bruce Adler a set of bongo drums for his birthday. "My parents never forgave her for that," Bruce said. "They got me an electric guitar — it was quieter!"

No Threatening Mudslides

Albert Brooks, who played Goldie Hawn's husband in *Private Benjamin*, moved into a new house in the San Fernando Valley. "It has five rooms and three have no furniture," he said. "I'm a slow mover."

I asked if he's threatened by the mudslides.

"Not personally," he said. "I haven't gotten any letters."

Albert Brooks

Speaking Without Sound

It is ironic that Israeli mime Eno has a father who speaks ten languages. "I went to the other extreme," he says. "I don't use any language." That is all right. Eno translates into all the languages of the world—in a quiet sort of way.

The Rabbi's a Cutup

Publicist Mike Hall's former assistant, Debbie Allen, got married and, two years later, was ready to give birth. So she called the rabbi to arrange for a possible *brit*.* But the temple informed her that the rabbi had left—to become a comedian.

"Come to think of it," Debbie said, "he was pretty funny at the wedding."

Just as well—circumcision is no laughing matter.

* Circumcision ceremony.

Also a Feminist

Nava Bodinger, a former tough-as-nails Israeli army officer, is a soft-spoken New York concert producer. Her husband, Herzl, is her road manager. They met in the army where she was a lieutenant and he was a private.

"I became a captain," she said. "He was still a private."

"But now at home," I suggested, "he's the general, right?"

"No," she said. "We're both equal."

Nava Bodinger

Comedian with a Mission

Robby Berman is a member of a unique club—he is an Orthodox comedian. As such, he brings a unique perspective to his shtick.

"I want to use my talent to enlighten people about their own religion and prevent intermarriage and assimilation."

That is a tall order, but he is aware of the obstacles.

"Many Jews are so ignorant of their history—they think the Dreyfus affair is a love story. They think the Ten Commandments is a Chinese menu. They think the most important contribution Jews have made to civilization over three thousand years is real estate developers."

It Doesn't Take a Dummy

Ventriloquist Stanley Burns was in Florida for a series of performances. He was invited on a television program where the audience is encouraged to paint. Stanley came on with his puppet, Beryl. He put a brush in Beryl's hand and painted a picture. "See," the host said, "even a dummy can paint." Stanley still isn't sure to whom the host was referring.

Stanley Burns and friend.

Keep Your Advice

Irving Berlin always refused to look at other writers' songs or advise other composers. This decision, according to columnist Earl Wilson, may stem from a request years before from playwright Moss Hart. He asked Berlin to look at a song written by Hart's father, who was not a professional songwriter but wrote songs as a hobby.

Berlin agreed to look at it and then told the elder Hart, "It's all right, but I'd suggest that here . . . ."

"Look, Irving Berlin," the old man exploded, "you write your songs the way you want to and I'll write my songs the way I want to!"

Fate of a Family

Frank Field, who has been in television broadcasting for thirty-eight years as medicine/science reporter and weatherman, took a camera crew to Poland to retrace his roots. He went to Dabrowice to learn the fate of the parents of his mother, Sarah Berkowitz.

He found an old man who recognized the Berkowitz family from photos Frank carried. He said he was a young man when the German SS ordered the Jewish villagers to evacuate their homes. The major told this young man, "You must take the Berkowitz family to the next town. They're going to put them in a ghetto."

The man said, "I got my wagon, put the children in—I used to play with them—and we went to Berenau."

The man led Field to the Berenau village square. He showed them where the Berkowitzes had put down their luggage.

"What happened to the family?" Field asked.

"The Germans told me to take them to a soccer field," the man said. He took Field into the woods and pointed out the spot where each person was made to sit down—and was shot.

"What was the worst part of this?" Field asked.

"The worst part," the man said, "was that the ground kept moving after they were shot. We had young Jewish men throw dirt over them. Then they were shot."

Field walked away, weeping.

Frank Field

*Mike Burstyn
and mom, Lillian Lux.*

Get Him to the Show
on Time

The biggest embarrassment of Mike Burstyn's professional life occurred thirty years ago when he was to perform at a New Year's Eve diplomat ball at the Tel Aviv Hilton.

His film, *Kuni Leml*, was then in the theaters, so he was even more popular than usual.

That day he had finished a week of children's shows and was exhausted. He was set to go on at the Hilton at one in the morning, so he figured he could get six hours sleep before the show. He disconnected the phone and set the alarm for midnight. When next he opened his eyes it was two o'clock in the morning. "I will never forget that feeling the rest of my life," he says.

His parents, Yiddish actors Pesach Burstein and Lillian Lux, had been trying to reach him. They could not get through. They called hospitals and police stations.

Mike rushed to the hotel. His costar, Chava Alberstein, had been singing encores for an extra hour, keeping the audience of eight hundred in their seats as long as she could. About a hundred people were left when Mike finally appeared.

Not only did the hotel not pay him, but it took fifteen years before management trusted him again. That's when the Hilton hired him to be the official spokesperson for the in-house television system in the guest rooms.

Today Mike travels with extra alarm clocks.

But Practice Makes Perfect

Richard Dreyfuss says he came to appreciate his religion late in life. He once asked his father, "Why don't we practice Judaism?"

"I don't have to practice," his father answered. "I'm very good at it."

Richard Dreyfuss

Getting Your Money's Worth

Myrna and Harvey Frommer, authors of *It Happened in the Catskills*, overheard a conversation in the Concord.

"Another meal?" a woman said. "We got to have another meal?"

"You don't have to eat," her husband said.

"But we're paying for it!"

Audition under the Chupah

The most memorable wedding Rabbi David Baron performed was the union of Richard and Rebecca Perry at Le Belage Hotel in Los Angeles. Richard had produced records for the Pointer Sisters and other artists, so among the wedding guests were a few celebrities.

Under the *chupah*, Cantor Judy Fox turned to Rabbi Baron and said, "I'm a little nervous."

"Why?" asked the rabbi.

"I never sang for Bette Midler and Elton John before," said the cantor.

Looking Good

Irving Berlin (left) with Fred Astaire.

Joe the barber had been cutting Irving Berlin's hair for forty-five years. He barbered Berlin for an Ed Sullivan television special.

When Berlin saw him afterward, Joe raved about the show, how his family, the neighbors, all loved it.

"And how did I do?" asked Berlin, who had stood up to sing.

"Mr. Berlin," exclaimed Joe, "your hair looked wonderful!"

Midnight Visitor

The Leon Street family helped found the Progressive Liberal Party of South Africa, which was in opposition to the apartheid government at the time.

A son, Paul, recalls having to leave his room in the middle of the night so Nelson Mandela could hide there. The Street family often hid him at great personal risk.

INDEX

A

Ace, Goodman, 66
Adler, Bruce, 25, 169, 255
Adler, Larry, 236
Adler, Leah, 210
Akim, 160
Albert Einstein College of Medicine, 179
Alda, Alan, 167
Aleichem, Sholom, 98, 213
Alexander, Jason, 173
Allen, Bernie, 82
Allyson, June, 72
Alony, Michael, 111
American Jewish Congress, 30, 36, 184
American Zionist Movement, 148
Amichai, Yehuda, 190
Anderson, Walter, 103
Angelescu, Jackie, 40
Anti-Defamation League, 17, 61, 108, 135, 221
Anzelowitz, Louis, 252
Appeal of Conscience Foundation, 119
Arbuse, Joan Goldberg, 249
Archer, Alexander, 76
Aridor, Yoram, 44, 247
Arlen, Harold, 28
Arthur, Bea, 90
Asimov, Isaac, 83, 126
Assaf Harofeh Medical Center, 142
Astaire, Fred, 63
Autrey, Gene, 88
Avital, Colette, 11, 107
Azrielant, Aya, 113, 165

B

Bacall, Lauren, 48
Bagel, Tom, 117
Baker, Blanche, 72
Baker, Carroll, 24, 49, 78
Baker, Ellen Shulman, 17
Ball, Lucille, 131
Bar-Ilan University, 83
Baron, David, 33, 261
Barry, Claire, 38, 130
Barry, Gene, 89, 251
Barton's, 156
Beame, Abe, 133
Bear Stearns, 168
Beatles, 10
Begin, Menachem, 100
Belafonte, Harry, 217
Belkin, Samuel, 179
Belzberg, Lisa, 189
Ben-David, Mordecai, 246
Ben-Gurion, David, 12, 23, 72, 91, 100, 118, 150,152, 155
Ben-Gurion University, 177, 191, 217
Ben-Meir, Yehuda, 74
Benny, Jack, 12, 236
Ben-Zvi, Yitzhak, 143
Berenstein, Rick, 254
Bergen, Polly, 251
Berger, Mendy, 183
Berke, Julie, 185
Berle, Milton, 23, 136, 197
Berlin, Irving, 258, 262

ABOUT THE AUTHOR

Tim Boxer currently covers the celebrity circuit for New York's *Jewish Week*. His column appears in Boston, Los Angeles, Orlando, and other major U.S. cities. He is also the arts and entertainment editor and gossip columnist for *Open Air PM*, New York's afternoon daily newspaper.

For twenty years Tim Boxer covered show business for *The New York Post*. He was assistant to syndicated Broadway columnist Earl Wilson, and after Wilson retired, Mr. Boxer wrote his own gossip column and then a television column for *The Post*. For two years he produced and hosted a television program of celebrity interviews on Manhattan Cable.

An accomplished photographer, the author's star photos have appeared in *Time*, *Life*, *Newsweek*, *Star*, *People*, and numerous other magazines around the world. He travels the lecture circuit with his Jewish Superstars of Hollywood slide show/lecture.

A native of Winnipeg, Canada, Tim Boxer's journalism career started at the City News Bureau of Chicago, where he was a police reporter. He was a feature writer for *The Sentinel*, Chicago's Jewish weekly. A former student of the Hebrew Theological College, the author now lives in Queens, New York, with his wife, Nina, and two sons, Gabriel and David.